Juan Sebastián Elcano

Juan Sebastián Elcano

You First Encircled Me

Bradley Thomas Angle

This book is a work of nonfiction. Names, characters, places, and incidents either are represented as per respected historical knowledge or are directly quoted/sourced from primary and secondary sources. Information which should be historically or academic authenticated is cited, with the exception of what is commonly known to scholars.

Produced by Dirty Sailor Company and Bradley Thomas Angle
Visit the website at www.dirtysailorcompany.com

Printed in the United States of America

First Printing: 2019

ISBN 9781695433786

This book is dedicated to Kristen.
For initiating a trip that changed my view of history.
For sharing time.
For reading under the volcanoes.

Introduction and Methodology

The Elcano Story is Layered, Political and Mostly Unknown.

...Because of hunger, sickness, and the ship's taking on water, some of the men wanted to put in at a Portuguese port called Mazambis. The others preferred to die rather than not return to Spain. Finally, with the help of God they passed within six leagues of the cape. Then for two months they sailed northwest continuously, without taking any rest. During this time twenty-one men died. And when they throw Christians into the sea, they sink to the bottom face up, and the Indians face down. And if God have not given them good weather, they would all have died of hunger.
—*The Voyage of Magellan, the journal of Antonio Pigafetta*

*E*ACH CHAPTER BEGINS WITH A QUOTE from the Journal of Antonio Pigafetta. It is, after all, the only visual account[1] of the great voyage, "Armada de Molucca," written by a participant of the entire journey. It is not, however, without its flaws, imaginations, and biases. That is, even as a primary source of history, it needs to be scrutinized, more so than it's been. This text is the most significant reason for the celebration of Ferdinand Magellan. This Journal has been the basis for the Heroic Tales of Magellan

---

[1] The Contramaestre (Boatswain) Francisco Albo, aboard the Trinidad and then the Victoria, kept a detailed log of the voyage in navigation terms. Which is to say, there is much information about location and little information about story, culture, or crew. This log and Pigafetta's are the two surviving documents from the Victoria.

for all of the Western World, and most of Europe, for the past 500 years! Sure, historians have tackled the subject. Their scrutiny has been deep and precise. Yes, yes; Historians can tell us something about Magellan. But even historians have their bias. Jesus! They/We still say "Columbus discovered America," or, "Magellan was the first to circumnavigate the world." But it is they, the writers of history, who also stubbornly admit that people were in the Americas before Columbus "discovered" it, and that Magellan didn't quite make that significant loop. We see, soon, that politics form the biases, politics overwhelm the accounts, and politics weave the supposed heroes of history into their supposed proper places.

The Journal of Pigafetta is only a layer. A single layer in the vast delicious cake of Juan Sebastián Elcano. After Pigafetta and Elcano, sixteen[2] men are the other significant accomplices of the journey. Most of whom, granted, could not read, much less write. These sixteen left their eye-witness accounts at the post circumnavigation trials. A handful of men would report to Maximilianus Transylvanus, who would in turn transcribe the first third-party account of the circumnavigation, titled: "De Moluccis Insulis."

In addition to these eye-witness accounts we have the testimony of up to two additional crew who made it back to Spain, after being captured by the Portuguese in Tidore, when their ship, the Trinidad, lost its seaworthiness. While these men did not complete the circumnavigation first, their stories are significant to demonstrate the mindsets of seaman during the expedition.

And there are more still. The mutineers of the San Antonio were awaiting in cold chains and captivity for the success or, more hopefully, failure of their Captain-General Magellan. The crew of the San Antonio had mutinied against Magellan in the South American straits – granted they didn't believe they were in the Straits at the time – and had returned to Spain, only to be thrown in prison due to lack of cohesive believability. These 55 crew members left an extremely complete look at the first two legs of the Armada de Molucca – from the first mutiny in North Africa, to the second Mutiny on

---

[2] 18 is the number who made it back to Spain alive, on the Victoria. The number who circumnavigated is closer to 26, though four of these men came back much later (years), as the ballast of Portuguese Men-of-war and merchant ships, and a hand full of men died after completing the first technical circumnavigation, near the Canary Islands.

the South American coast. They left a record so complete, we are able to piece together precision locations and routes of the fleet, even though it happened five centuries ago. Yes, these 55 men were confessing under duress, and surely lied for their own cause, but they were healthy when they returned, compared to the starving men of the Victoria.

∞ ∞ ∞

SPAIN CELEBRATES JUAN SEBASTIÁN ELCANO. They celebrate the man, his family, and his voyage. The man, is celebrated in bronze, in history, and in literature – literature that is, to this day, not translated outside of Spanish[3]. His family, well at least his children born out of wedlock (seems like Elcano wasn't the most faithful, truthful, or stable to the ladies), were all taken care of, as the nobles and land holders of the Negros Islands in the Philippines. To this day, the Elcano family name is the largest in the area. And the voyage, is Juan Sebastián's Voyage; Spain does not refer to Magellan as we do. The "Armada de Molucca" was Juan Sebastián Elcano's expedition. The final leader, in all truth and good history, overcame some of the most daunting hardships anyone has ever encountered, and he did it for Spain, for the honour of his King, out of contract, and smartly.

Spain celebrates for obvious reasons. Their choice of Elcano over Magellan is natural. Magellan was Portuguese. Elcano was Spanish. But their choice is political too. The Spanish were always getting the floppy end of the stick in European social circles. The Portuguese were wowing the world back-to-back with their Navigational successes, and they had been since 1488, when Bartolomeu Dias sailed around Cape Hope. Then, in 1498, Vasco de Gama sailed all the way to India. The English were kicking butt on the European fronts. The Italians were notable for the Renaissance – their

---

[3] Not until this book. Also, see "Juan Sebastián Elcano: la Mayor Travesía de la Historia"

9

culture, art, and production of scholars. While their politics were crumbling, their societies were the envy of Europe. The Moors because they were The Infamous Enemy. And the French, under King Francis 1, was overwhelmed by the sheer economic power of the surrounding countries. Francis 1 promoted the ideals of the Italian Renaissance, but he allied with the Protestants of England and the Moors from Africa and the Middle East. With the spinning competition in Europe, Spain was in no place to celebrate a Portuguese progeny. Magellan was no Hero for Spain. Juan Sebastián Elcano was their man.

∞ ∞ ∞

HE METHODOLOGIES USED TO COMPLETE this book are not 100 percent scholarly. But don't be disappointed, this is not a fictitious history either. It's not a poetic narrative, nor a required project for Yale[4]. As we move forward in our story of Elcano, it needs to be stated upfront that we didn't have all the answers and detail. Like narrative histories, this story is fluffed where it could be, and vacant where there was nothing to fluff. Though, a majority is taken from those layers mentioned earlier and the rest is scalped from other researchers, our favorite historians, and students who thankfully have published the research of others. This text leans most heavily on Pigafetta, Maximilianus and a collection of secondary resources (all cited in text and within the bibliography and the end of the book). But this text is also written by a mariner, with 20 years of seagoing experience, a USCG licensed Captain, and a academic from the California State Universities, with degrees in behavioral science and history. Where historical evidence lacks, professional inference is inserted.

---

[4] Through studying different historical figures, I've noticed that many half-assed student projects from Yale are published by Yale publishing.

The different versions of the Voyage of Magellan, at least the accounts of the different heroes, are amazing. A comprehensive analysis leaves us wondering who was in the legal right, who were the mutineers, who held loyalties to who. Magellan was not a Saint in this mess. He abandoned the Portuguese crown –he was even hunted by the Portuguese as his fleet of five ships left Spain. And, as some of the mutineers reported it, his ultimate and secret goal was not in line with that of the Spain. Many of his fellow officers and crew suspected the worse before they left home. But we will never know for certain. If you want a more detailed look into the story of Magellan, with a pro Magellan spirit, there are countless accounts available. This book touches on those accounts, as he was the Captain-General Juan Sebastián worked under for half of the journey, but this book's main focus is the Elcano story. Perhaps both accounts carry much political truth.

$\mathcal{T}$O GET IT OUT OF THE WAY: many versions of Juan Sebastián Elcano's name can be found in various text and online sources. Del Cano, for example, is a popular one. From my research, specifically through the article in the footnotes[5], the proper name, using a systematic and well-thought-out look into the matter, is Juan Sebastián Elcano. The use of only "Juan" is incorrect for Basque names of the time, though "Juan Sebastián" is correct. The use of Elcano alone is also correct. You will read both "Juan Sebastián" and "Elcano" in this text.

---

[5] S. Múgica.— Elcano Y No Cano

PRIMUS CIRCUMDEDISTI ME
(YOU FIRST ENCIRCLED ME)
—Inscription on Elcano's Family's Coast of Arms,
Authorized by the Holy Roman Emperor Charles V

Contents

Introduction and Methodology 7

Historical or Political Perspective 17

Age of Exploration 21

Key Persons 25

Elcano 31

Under the Traitor 37

The Passage 51

Crossing the Pacific 57

Magellan's Success 65

Magellan's Death 69

Crossing the Indian 79

Circumnavigation Complete 87

Hero Elcano 89

The End 93

The First Eighteen 95

Bibliography 97

About the Author 101

Historical or Political Perspective

Magellan, Slave, Elcano, Who else?

The voyage and exploration of the Spaniards among the Moluccas, the islands that they found during said voyage, the Kings of these islands, their governments and manner of living, together with many other things.
—Antonio Pigafetta, his Introduction to his Journal

THE FIRST PERSON TO CIRCUMNAVIAGTE the world was not Ferdinand Magellan, at least, in due probability it was not Magellan. And it was not Magellan's servant, Enrique of Malacca. What we know about these two men and their geographical whereabouts through time is mostly complete. Magellan, in 1505 to 1513, made multiple voyages on Portuguese trading vessels and war ships, spent time in Indian and Malaysia, purchased a slave named Enrique, and returned to Portugal. He then sold his ideas to Spain, to reach the Spice Islands by sailing West, like Columbus, and he almost did so, reaching Cebu, Philippines in 1521, and dying there. The distance between Magellan's furthest point East with Portugal, Malaysia, and his furthest point West, with Spain, the Philippines, lacks circumnavigation by 1500 miles. Sorry, historians mostly agree that Magellan was not the first to circumnavigate. In a similar, and maybe just as important, claim, Enrique, Magellan's servant/slave did not make a complete venture around the globe. It seems that he made it further than

Magellan, though historians are skeptical that he completed the journey, as he stopped at Cebu, like Magellan, and was most probably from Sumatra, as slaves were sold from that region and his spoken language did not overlap the Philippian's fluidly. Enrique would have been nearly 1000 miles short of circumnavigation.

With Magellan and Enrique out of the equation, who then are the remaining candidates, of first person to circumnavigate the world? The answer is not one man. The answer is the crew of the Spanish Carrack Victoria, the one ship of the Spanish Armada de Molucca to complete the circumnavigation. These men experienced something quite unfathomable for their day, and completely incomprehensible for us in the 21st century. The recognition for their efforts and successes needs to be spread amongst them. As for my subtitle, Juan Sebastián Elcano was indeed the only Captain on the Victoria, and in certain context, it would make sense to give him the honors. Though this title is misleading, and should not signify his superiority amongst the great seafarers of the world. As few historians have pointed out, the higher recognition for seafarer of the early 16th century should go to all of the men aboard the Victoria who completed the circumnavigation. Because the Victoria overlapped the first and last 900 miles of their journey, the crew onboard at the point of passing the Canary Islands are the first – and however many, and who died, from that point to landfall in Spain, is uncertain at best (but roughly two people). The 18 crew who made Spanish landfall alive and recorded their names are listed at the end of this book.

∞ ∞ ∞

CAPTAIN JUAN SEBASTIÁN ELCANO was truly a good navigator, a successful expeditionary, and a man to be recognized. Though Elcano is correctly placed as second to Magellan in gallant form, as the Americas view it. And he is incorrectly, though necessarily, placed as a hero in Spanish rhetoric. The Americans point to the multiple hardships that Magellan overcame, as he sailed *unknown* waters, in an *unknown part of the world*, for longer than any other captain-general. Juan Sebastián, conquered a lot, yes, but he was a trader to his captain, and in doing so he may have insulted the Spanish Crown (if he was incorrect about Magellan's motives) – but Spain needed(needs) to claim Juan Sebastián regardless.

$$\infty \quad \infty \quad \infty$$

T—HIS IS THE STORY OF CAPTAIN JUAN SEBASTIÁN ELCANO. We begin with the man, born to a torn world of heavy politics, religion, and economic divides. We move to the great start, from Seville, across the Atlantic under the leadership of a known traitor[6], a Portuguese Captain, Ferdinand Magellan. Then into the prison aboard his own ship, as it sailed towards and through unknown straits and into an unknown ocean of unknown lengths. Through hunger, mania, and hallucinations. Finally reaching land, first in Guam and shortly after the Philippines. To witnessing the death and destruction of their leader, and the ironic salvation of his own honor. Then to the great voyage home, to the Spice Islands, across twenty-thousand miles of sea infested with enemies, disease, storm, and hunger. To his successful landing, back in Sanlúcar de Barrameda Spain.

Once a hero, he was sent again, to the Spice Islands, via the same route Magellan had gone. Here, in the Pacific Ocean, is the ending of the man. Though his story has lived on, and his influence has stretched the globe.

---

[6] Again, this has been stated multiple times though its point is truly important, Ferdinand Magellan betrayed his own King, Manuel I, and many officers aboard the Armada de Molucca distrusted Magellan as a person, and they distrusted him as a possible spy who had taken advantage of their 18 year old kind, King Charles I.

Age of Exploration

15th/16th Century Globalization

Each one of the live according to his own wishes, having no
king. They go about naked, and some wear beards, black hair,
tied at the waist. They wear hats made of palm leaves, like the
Albanians. They are of our stature, and are well-formed, of an
olive color, but they are born white. Their teeth are red and
black, and they consider this to be very attractive. And they do
not worship anything.
—*Antonio Pigafetta*

HE FIRST VOYAGE TO PURPOSEFULY set sail west, "around the globe," was of course under the direction of the man who would become known to be "The Admiral of the Ocean Sea," Christopher Columbus. This was in 1492. Columbus was only attempting to solve the maritime puzzle that was tormenting most of Europe, and benefitting only Portugal. Thanks to Vasco De Gama, a Portuguese navigator following the schooling set by The Prince of Navigation – Prince Henry, son of King John of Portugal, 1419, the Portuguese had final "found" a route around Africa to India, and then naturally further to the known Spice Islands[7]. The Silk Roads had been open for centuries, and Spices were the measurement of success for all of Europe. Whomever had the spices, had the

---

[7] Arabian traders had a stronghold over the spice trade – which typically followed the Norther Indian Oceans, the Red Sea, and routes across land, through Egypt of Istanbul, before reaching trading posts in the Mediterranean. Finding water routes to the Spice Islands completely removed the middle man – the Arabs.

wealth and the power[8]. Portugal was that power from 1498 through the early 16th century, because Portugal had discovered, established, and fortified the sea routes to the Spice Islands first. Later, thanks to Columbus opening an entire new territory, the Catholic Pope Alexander VI established a boundary for his two subjects, Spain and Portugal, to coexist by. "1494's Treaty of Tordesillas," a decree from Pope Alexander VI that had essentially divided the world in half between the Spanish and the Portuguese. This agreement placed the more practical eastern route to the Spice Islands under Portuguese control, forcing the Spanish to find a new passage by sailing west through South America. This new line further prevented Spaniards and other Europeans to travel to the Spice Islands via Cape Hope, Africa, and the Portuguese continued their monopoly over spices. Though, not all was bad. A series of Ocean crossing had taken place soon after Columbus returned and both the Spanish and Portuguese were poking and prodding, raping and pillaging, the "new" lands they were "discovering." Again, the Pope's Treaty of Tordesillas split this land in twain, well at least that was the attempt, to prevent Spain and Portugal from fighting. All land East of a longitude, 100 leagues west of Cape Verde, would be given to Portugal. This included strongholds on Malaysia (at least in the theory of the moment), and all land west of that longitude would be for Spain[9]. This is why Brazil is divided the way it is.

In other parts of Europe, wars were spinning. Italy was breaking apart and both civil wars and hostile invasions were opening opportunities for European nations to prove their dominance. Spain, England, France, the Ottoman Empire, and the Moors[10] were fighting over Italian real-estate. The Italian wars would last for 50 years.

The Crusades were still happening in the 16th century. And along with the Crusades, the Christian Wars were happening as well – between orthodox Catholics and more progressive sects, and other groups of Christians

---

[8] A sock stuffed with cloves or cinnamon would be sufficient for any sailor to retire. The value of Spices came from the Noble class, who used them to flavor the horrible food of the day, for medicinal purposes, and as displays of status.

[9] This line moved multiple times, based on influence, regime changes, and discovery.

[10] I use the term "Moors" to encompass Muslims in both North Africa and along common trade routes.

protesting the Vatican's control. Amongst these Christians wars were the Catholic Inquisitions, and then the more developed Spanish Inquisition. This method of spotlighting subpar Catholics, or just non-Catholics, and then torturing them until they reached the afterlife, was fresh on Juan Sebastián's mind. It was also fresh in the fleet of the Armada de Moluccas, as we will see.

The Italian Renaissance was in full swing. And when there was breathing room between killing each other, there was a large movement for public education, art and science. The Italians were the scholars of the World, and they had a deep history they were uncovering and promoting. Antonio Pigafetta was a member of this mindset. He volunteered to go with the Armada de Molucca, only to document such a trip, for its anthropologic value and its scientific appeal. As an Italian scholar, his goal was to become famous as the voyage's transcriber.

Like the Renaissance, pulling Europe out of the Dark Ages, the protestant reformation was looking at humanity in a new light. The mostly English participants in the protest of the Catholic Church were against the Inquisition. Their demands for religious freedoms, and for freedoms to interpret the words of God, would lead to even more death a destruction across Europe. And that death and destruction, unfortunately for the natives, was dragged into the Americas, by Spanish, Portuguese and English explorers, merchants, and noblemen.

The class system in Europe, specifically Spain, was still intact from the Medieval/Early Modern European era. Individual welfare and social status were mostly a direct cause of who you were born to and where you were born. The noble elite were the monarchy and close families. The next tier down were the landowners. And then the business men. Everyone else was a peasant. It is important to distinguish the cultural developments that happened separately between each class. Each cultural feature, in each class distinction, played a direct role on survival probability during the circumnavigation. Moving back to the social divides, both developments in agriculture and urbanization, led to huge gains for all classes, and then huge losses for the lower classes. Disease and epidemics often hit the lower class hard, and not so much the upper classes, due to nutritional intake alone[11]. The upper classes had access to vitamins (as we'll see on our voyage) that the peasant class did not. This malnutrition lead to a constant and reoccurring problem for the lower class. Not only is it hard to provide for your family when you're sick and/or dead, but it is hard to learn and develop your body and brain as you grow through your adolescence. Without taking into account tuberculosis, syphilis, and leprosy, which were all too common in the 16th century, famine alone accounted for the demise and noticeable class distinction throughout the peasant class of European history. This social phenomenon carried itself aboard the five ships of the Armada de Molucca, and it explains the survival of the Officers in the Pacific, and then the survival of the seamen in Asia. It also shows how Juan Sebastián Elcano was able to slide into the leadership role in a moment of relative chaos.

.

---

[11] Malnutrition along, throughout the centuries, accounts for the inability to rise in social status. Rickets was wide spread in the 16th century peasant class, causing bone deformity and brain trauma.

Key Persons

A list of significant characters

Fernan de Magalhães would not make any further stay, and at
once set sail, and ordered the course to be steered west.
—Antonio Pigafetta

Alexander VI, Pope: (1431 – 1503): Spain. Catholic Pope from 1492 to 1503. Established the Treaty of Tordesillas in 1494, diving the New World between Spain and Portugal, and giving Portugal rights to the known sea routes around Cape Hope.

Álvaro de Mesquita (????): Portugal. Cousin(friend) of Ferdinand Magellan. Later, captain of the San Antonio. Taken hostage by his crew and returned to Spain before the Armada made safe passage through the Straits of Magellan. Mesquita was held in a dungeon until the Victoria returned. (Most of the crew of the San Antonio were also held until their stories could be corroborated.) The San Antonio arrived in Spain as the Victoria was leaving Tidore.

Antonio Pigafetta: (1491 – 1531): Venice, Italy. Journalist. Loyal to Magellan. Published a second edition of his Journal: Il Primo Viaggio Intorno al Mondo (The first trip around the world), after he gave his original journal to King Charles V upon his return from the expedition.

Antonio Salmon: (???? – 1519): First crew member to be tried and hung. Salmon was the pilot aboard the Victoria, under Mendoza. He was found guilty of sodomy (with a cabin-boy) and hung in the rigging, while the fleet was anchored in Rio de Janeiro.

Antonio de Coca: (???): Spain. Pilot of the San Antonio, under Juan de Cartagena. Called on by Magellan to replace Antonio Salmon, then to replace Juan de Cartagena. Coca is then replaced by Mesquita for either charges of mutiny or failure to manage his ship properly.

Ambrosio Fernandes. (????): Spain (most likely). Chief Constable for the Armada de Molucca. Executed the mutineer Luis de Mendoza, aboard the Victoria in Saint Julian, which was the key maneuver for Magellan's victory over that mutiny.

Archbishop Juan Rodriguez de Fonseca: (1451 – 1524): Zamora, Spain. Catholic head of trade for Spain. As the presiding authority of the Casa de Contratación he influenced both the Christopher Columbus and Ferdinand Magellan contracts on behalf of the State. Managed Native America affairs, specifically ethical affairs (unfortunately for the Native Americans). Served as the President on the Council of the Indies, after Juan Sebastián Elcano's return. Also, coincidentally perhaps, was the signature Juan Sebastián Elcano needed to receive a pardon from King Charles, and to join the Armada de Molucca.

Cardinal Fray Francisco Jimenez de Cisneros, Archbishop of Toldeo:(1436 – 1517): A prominent figure in Spanish, European and Catholic politics. He led armies to defeat the Moors in North Africa, where he would have met Juan Sebastián Elcano. Most notably he argued with Archbishop Juan Rodriguez de Fonseca over the treatment of heathens in the Americas. Having served the Archbishop was a major selling point for Juan Sebastián, in his criminal pardons at Seville.

Duarte Barbosa (??? – 1521): Portugal. Experienced mariner and friend of Magellan's. Took control of the Armada after Magellan's death, alongside Serrano. Murder by the King of Cebu, while the entire fleet watched from the ships a hundred feet off shore.

Esteban Gómez: (1483 – 1538): Portugal. Mariner and cartographer. Mutinied in the Straits of Magellan and sailed the San Antonio back to Spain. Arrested and put on trial when the Victoria arrived two years later. Released to sail for Spain again. Died at sea.

Enrique of Malacca: (1497 - ????): Sumatra, Indonesia. Slave purchased by Magellan during the Portuguese crusade to Malaysia. Enrique most likely did not make it all the way around the globe. He was last seen on the beach at Cebu, during the battle there. Many accounts suggest Enrique sabotaged the mission, as he was the obviously upset by the treatment of Duarte Barbosa and Francisco Serrao following Magellan's death.

Ferdinand Magellan: (1480 – 1521): Sabrosa, Portugal. Portuguese Nobility. Superb mariner and navigator. Participated in two Portuguese crusades to the Malaccas, on the Malaysian Peninsula (South of Thailand and North of Singapore). Decorated and wounded war hero. Later signed contract with King Charles of Spain, to use his knowledge gained from Portugal to sail east to the Spice Islands. Original Captain-General of the Armada de Molucca.

Francisco Albo: (????): Rhodes, Greece. Hired as master-at-arms aboard Magellan's ship, Trinidad. Later, worked under Juan Sebastián Elcano as pilot. Albo's detailed log, containing coordinates and navigational information is one of two surviving account of the circumnavigation.

Gaspar de Quesada: (14?? – 1520): Seville, Spain. Captain of the Concepción. Loyalty to the Archbishop Juan Rodriguez de Fonseca is documented in letters written before the expedition. Mutinied against Magellan, in conjunction with other Spanish officers, including Juan de Cartagena. Tried and sentenced to death alongside Luis de Mendoza.

Ginés de Mafra: (1493–1546): Spain/Portugal. Crew aboard the Trinidad when it was arrested by the Portuguese in the Moluccas. Survived over two years after his arrest, in captivity in both India and aboard Portuguese men-of-war. Jailed after returning to Spain. Historians believe he had copies of important documents of Magellan's, though none of these exist today.

Gonzalo Gomez de Espinosa: (1479-1530): The loyal Master-at-Arms of Magellan's. Helped squelch the mutiny in St. Julian. Fought beside Magellan at the battle of Mactan. Took charge of the Armada de Moluccas after the leading pilot, Carvalho failed to manage the fleet.

Juan de Cartagena, Inspector General: (14?? – 1520). Seville, Spain. Illegitimate son of Archbishop Juan Rodriguez de Fonseca. Without any skills or experience, it was ill fortune for Magellan that this man was placed as second in command of the fleet. Magellan, in a show of submission and gratitude, place Cartagena as Captain of the largest ship, San Antonia. Cartagena would lead two mutinies during the first year of the expedition. He would later be marooned, on a uninhabited and desolate small island just off of Patagonia – never to be seen again.

Juan Sebastián Elcano (1486 – 1526): Getaria, Spain (Basque). Family was business class, in maritime trade. Army officer in Italian wars. Officer in North African crusades. Maritime business owner in Seville. Arrested and jailed. Negotiated a pardon from King Charles in exchange for joining the Armada de Molucca. Completed the circumnavigation with 17 crew and 4 slaves, as the captain. Died of scurvy on his second attempt to reach the Moluccas.

João Rodrigues Serrão (Juan Serrano): (14?? – 1521): Portugal. Captain of the Santiago. Cousin of Ferdinand Magellan. Served in Portuguese conquest of the Malaysian Peninsula with his brother and Magellan in early 16th century. Planned to meet his brother in the Spice Islands. Died on beach in Cebu, shortly after Magellan's death in Mactan days earlier.

Joao Lopez Carvalho: (???? – 1521): Spain: Captain-General of the three remaining ships after Balboa and Serrano were murdered. Ordered the scuttling of the Conception in the Philippines and sailed the fleet randomly to Brunei. Relieved of his duties by Espinosa when he failed at managing the fleet, leading many men and his own son to die in unnecessary conflict with Muslim spice traders.

King Charles / Charles I / Charles V, Holy Roman Emperor: (1500 – 1558): Castile Spain. King Charles I of Spain, at age 18. First allotted Magellan five ships and authority to sail under the Spanish Flag. Later crowned Holy Roman Emperor, as Charles V.

Luis de Mendoza, General Treasurer: (14?? – 1520): Captain of the Victoria. Participated in mutiny, under orders of Juan de Cartagena. Was arrested and strangled and quartered by Magellan in Saint Julian, in January 1520.

Luis Molino: Squire aboard the San Antonio, under command of Gaspar de Quesada. Convicted of mutiny. His sentence was suspended, in exchange he was required to carry out the torture of his superior, Quesada, which he did.

Maximilianus Transylvanus (1490 – 1538): Nobleman, serving King Charles V. Ordered by the King to take a detailed report from the survivors of the circumnavigation. Within a few days he published "de moluccis insulis" (the Molucca Islands), which was a brief account of the entire Armada de Molucca. It is one of the best sources historians have of the expedition.

Elcano

Before 1516

When any of these three fish encounter any of these flying fish,
the flying fish immediately leap out of the water and fly as far
as a bowshot without wetting their winds. And the other fish
dart under the shadows of the flying fish, and no sooner do they
fall into the water, than they are immediately seized and eaten.
— Antonio Pigafetta

HE WAS BORN A BASQUES, IN GETARIA, SPAIN, in 1486, six years before an Italian under the name Columbus would sail for the Spanish Crown, West, to the Indies. Elcano soon was sailing with his brothers in the shipping industry, ferrying goods from the Bay of Biscay to and from France. It was in this environment, alone with his very catholic brothers – one of which later became a Catholic priest – and exposed to everything nautical, that Elcano developed the skillset that would save the crew of the only ship of the Armada de Molucca, to complete the first circumnavigation.

Wanting to move away from the stagnant life aboard cargo transport, Elcano joined the Spanish Army and shipped to Italy to fight for Spanish and Catholic supremacy in the Italian Wars. It is here that Elcano moved from the business class into the officer/military class and it was here that he developed a habit of spending more money than he should. It was also in the Spanish Army that Elcano would work under the brutal Archbishop of Toldeo, Cardinal Fray Francisco Jimenez de Cisneros. With Jimenez, Elcano would fight again for the Spanish in Northern Africa, successfully killing, torturing and chasing off the Moors in that region.

By the end of the Archbishop's war in North Africa, Elcano was ready to retire from military life and he purchased and operated a merchant ship out of Seville. Soon he found himself between a rock and a hard place. Italian bankers had privateered[12] Elcano's ship and had negotiated an agreement with Elcano – in exchange for the ship, all of Elcano's debts would be forgiven. Unfortunately for Elcano, the deal was illegal, as Spanish law forbade merchants from surrendering their ships to the enemies (Italians) specifically when no aggressive defense was first made. Elcano's prospects of jail were very real.

Thanks to his social status and connections he made as an Army Officer, Juan Sebastián was able to negotiate a release from criminal charges through the Casa de Contratación – literally the House of Trades – which was the political and legal authority of matters of finance, trade, and the maritime. The Casa de Contratación worked directly with King Charles[13] for a pardon, in exchange, Juan Sebastián would take an insignificant role as an officer under Ferdinand Magellan in the Armada de Molucca.

The social connections Juan Sebastián had paint a clear portrait for us, showing Juan Sebastián's most likely loyalties from the start.

The key figure at the Casa de Contratación – the Spanish Government entity that worked Elcano's pardon through King Charles – was the Archbishop Juan Rodriguez de Fonseca. Fonseca had a previous working relationship with the Archbishop of Toledo, Cardinal Fray Francisco Jimenez de Cisneros, who Elcano fought for in both Italy and North Africa. These two Archbishops were very well informed of the condition of the Spanish front in South America. They not only were well informed, they were leading politicians (obviously they were central figures in the Catholic church as well) over the disputes of how to treat Native Americans, disputes on shipping and land rights, and disputes over merchant and lender privileges to cargo. Fonseca had access to the ear of the 18-year-old King, King Charles I. For strategic reasons, not only did he encourage the King to accept

---

[12] The Genoese bankers literally placed a lean on Elcano's ship, and then took it out from under his feet.

[13] Later, Emperor Charles V

Magellan's offer (to use his knowledge from his experience and information collected as an officer in the Portuguese Navy) but he fought for strategic positions amongst Magellan's fleet. This included educated and noble men, that could be controlled, like Elcano. Elcano's barter to avoid prison include consigning himself to the control of this to Archbishop – who, also coincidently, was a personal investor of the journey.

Another friend of the Archbishop in charge of the Casa de Contratación was Juan de Cartagena. And the term "friend" here means illegitimate son. As the spoiled offspring of high-ranking Catholic clergy, Fonseca, Caratagena needed a position that allowed for social prestige. His father used his power to ensure Caratagena would be placed in an easy position for this. With a bit of pressure, Fonseca ensured part of the Magellan deal included his son's status as second in command, the "Inspector General" slightly under Magellan.

So, over the roughly 250 crew that left from Seville, we know that nearly a dozen had direct ties to the Spanish entity that allowed and established financial backing for the journey to exist. One was Juan de Cartagena, an invalid within the maritime, and the illegitimate son of the Archbishop Juan Rodriguez de Fonseca. And the second, Juan Sebastián Elcano. Indebted to Fonseca. The others appear throughout the story – sharing one common attribute – they were the perpetrators of the mutinies in the Atlantic and at St. Julian. They were also not ashore during the battles of Mactan or Cebu.

RESTING ON THE BANKS of the Guadalquivir River, in the center of Seville, Magellan's five ships were busy with last second repairs and orders. Also, a number of people were busy with plans to sabotage Magellan...

With an already successful and monopolized route to the Spice Islands, Portugal actually had lots to lose by the discovery of a second route to that place. When Magellan made his offer, King Manuel I, of Portugal, was wise to decline. When Magellan refused to share his prized chart[14], which included the location of the passage through the New World, the King had placed spies on Magellan to ensure his plans never materialized. When the spies returned with news that Magellan had won over King Charles of Spain, King Emanuel was irate[15]. He immediately sent orders to the Portuguese Diplomats in Seville to squash Magellan's expedition before it started.

Meanwhile, the officers of the voyages were selected and paired up. Those in charge were given their said ships, and Magellan saw to it his second in command, Cartagena, was to be placed on the largest ship in the fleet. Magellan's own Juan Serrano would be given command of the third, The Santiago, and two other Castilians, Gaspar de Quesada and Luis de Mendoza would be on the fourth and fifth ship, the Conception and Victoria, respectively. Magellan himself would captain his own vessel, the Trinidad. As these officers went about their duties, Magellan was nearby, overly, but in necessity, scrutinizing every action and every movement aboard each vessel. The nosy Portuguese defector was too much for the prideful Castilians and soon rumors were stirring that Magellan was probably a spy, or double agent. Rumors spread that Magellan's chart was a forgery, a fraud, or simply non-existent.

Poking at this animosity building up between three of expedition's high-ranking officers, the Portuguese ambassador made things worse. He inflamed the rumors, talked poorly about Magellan, and suggested that perhaps there was an even larger plot afoot, that Magellan would disown Spain the moment they were clear of Spanish territory – after all, many of the officers and crew were not of Spanish origin[16].

Juan Sebastián was stationed on the San Antonio, the same ship as Cartagena, and would have encountered these rumors daily, from his

---

[14] Magellan claimed that he had a secret chart/knowledge to the passage that lead to the Pacific Ocean (The Pacific was "discovered" in 1513 by Vasco Núñez de Balboa). There is no evidence this knowledge existed, or if it did, was of any use. Magellan's route shows a desperate man searching, and not a proven navigator on target.

[15] The Portuguese never learned their lessons from Christopher Columbus, who was an Italian Mariner, who begged the Portuguese for help financing a similar trip. Columbus would find his funding through Spain, just like Magellan.

[16] In fact, ten countries of origin were represented aboard the Armada de Moluccas. This was not abnormal for the times, as talented seafarers were hard to come by.

Captain, from the diplomat from Portugal, and from the fellow Spanish officers. From Basque, his Spanish heritage would have held him higher than the non-Spaniards, though he still would have been considered lower blood than the other Spaniards, the Castilians.

At this point neither Elcano or Cartagena knew that they would be separated before departing Spain, and only their short voyage down the Guadalquivir River, from Seville to Sanlúcar de Barrameda, would be spent together. It was also at this point that Magellan took a management move that surprised his officers, he began hiring crew for his ships, all 200 of them. Amongst this group of people, he would hire seaman from over ten different countries. Historians seem to agree that this was only due to the supply of mariner available, and not some other reason, though, none-the-less, the Spanish officers in the fleet, Elcano included, would have been more comfortable with only other Spaniards. Amongst the crew were many members from Portugal, including close ties of Magellan's – officers and seaman.

Portuguese attacks from his left and signs of pending mutiny from his right, Magellan was in a bad spot. Juan Sebastián and his fellow Spanish officers knew this, and the opportunity to upend their Captain-General and seize the expedition for themselves had arrived. Then, suddenly, Magellan gave sudden orders. On August 10, 1519, to set sail and regroup at the end of the Guadalquivir River, at the Atlantic port of Sanlúcar de Barrameda, on the gulf of Cadiz. Cartagena approached his officers and began planning the logistics to have Magellan arrested.

The crews of the five ships would have been resigned to staying aboard their vessels while navigating the skinny and long river. Once at their destination, the work would continue to outfit the ships with stores and supplies needed to cross the Atlantic. Though the crews would have been restricted to ship work, the officers would have been free to move about as they saw fit. And this is what they all did: Magellan and Cartagena both rushed off, to either spread rumors or defend against them. Juan Sebastián took the opportunity to visit his favorite women and prostitutes, hopefully not impregnating any of them, this time.

Cartagena won an argument with the Casa de Contratación, and Magellan was order to replace a majority of his Portuguese crew with other seamen.

As a clever leader, Magellan used the opportunity to recruit new seamen, and stir up the shipping orders. Without any feedback from his officers, the Captain-General had stripped his Captain's their authority of choosing their own subordinates.

Of the five vessels, each had roughly fifty souls onboard. Of these, ten percent were officers. Magellan left the superior officer to his ship, and had the subordinate officers and lower ranking crews mixed. This action was no small deal and many ship's Masters refused. After much hysteria, Magellan held firm to his wishes. Juan Sebastián and Cartagena would not be sailing together, the plans to overthrow the Captain-General would have to be rushed. An agreement between the Spanish officers to meet the following week was established. They were confidant Magellan was a trader, despite his oath to their King.

Under the Traitor

Crossing the Atlantic: 1516

*The masters and captains of the others ships of his company did
not love him: of this I do not know the reason, except by cause of
his, the captain-general, being Portuguese, and they were
Spaniards or Castilians, who for a long time have been in
rivalry and ill will with one another.*
—Antony Pigafetta

HE GAVE THE ORDER TO MUSTER, ALL HANDS. The following day, on September the 20th, 1519, the confused and angry Captains cast off their mooring lines, and followed orders to regroup at the Canary Islands, the same Spanish outpost Columbus used 30 years earlier. As they set sail, Juan Sebastián leaned over the aft rail of the Concepción, captained by the Master Gaspar de Quesada, and watched Magellan oversee the dispersing ships. They had left so quickly; carts and kegs of supplies were still waiting on the piers.

Between 240 and 280 men were now at sea. The countries of Spain, Portugal, Italy, Germany, Belgium, Greece, England and France were represented among those men. The Spanish of course outnumbering the rest.

Aboard the Trinidad, a three masted carrack, or Nao, was the Captain-General of the fleet, Ferdinand Magellan. Magellan traveled with many close associates, including the paid journalist of the expedition, Antonio Pigafetta. His cousin Serrano was captaining the Santiago. Ashore, his father-in-law and other family were well aware of the political turmoil and the plot to sabotage Magellan.

The largest ship in the fleet was commanded by the second in command, Juan de Cartagena. Cartagena was irate that the Captain-General issued sailing orders without consulting him first. This meant his plans to overthrow the Captain-General would have to wait.

Without his allied officers onboard, like Juan Sebastián, Cartagena was forced to communicate through signaling, which often required the ships to sail dangerously close to one another. Aboard the San Antonio, the largest ship of the fleet, also a Carrack, weighing nearly 120 tons, Cartagena felt entitled. As the son of a powerful Archbishop, he felt untouchable. He gave signals often to other vessels, giving orders and direction without consulting with Magellan.

The third ship of the fleet, in size, was Concepción. As we know, she was mastered by another Spanish captain, Gaspar de Quesada, loyal to both Spain and Cartagena. Juan Sebastián was aboard this vessel, and as she made way, for the short 900-mile voyage to the Canary Islands, Elcano and Quesada, continued the discussion of the overthrow of Magellan. Whenever the San Antonia would come near, a signal would be given to adjust course, to gain speed advantage of the ships behind them, to leave Magellan behind the horizon.

Ship number four was the Santiago, captained by the Portuguese Pilot João Serrano. Despite the other officer's solicitation to rid all officers of non-Spanish blood from the voyage, the Casa de Contratación allowed for Juan Serrano, at Magellan's request, as, like Magellan, Juan Serrano also had experience in the Spice Islands. In fact, Serrano had made the voyage from Europe to the Spice Islands, around the Cape of Good Hope, more than once, and he would be one of the strongest and most experienced assets for the expedition. Little did the Spanish Crown know, Juan Serrano actually had a brother living in the Moluccas, which both Magellan and Serrano had the intention of meeting.

The final and smallest ship, the Victoria, was captained by another Spaniard, Luis de Mendoza, and piloted by Antonio Salmon. Mendoza and Juan Sebastián had been introduced by none other than the Portuguese diplomat in Seville. And while the two had not spent much time together, they were both fond of the night life, and had mingled with the same crowd in Sanlúcar de Barrameda.

These five vessels pushed tons of water out of their way as they sailed towards their outpost at Tenerife[17]. Once there, orders were issued to resupply, water being the priority. The routes to the Americas were well charted at this point, and this armada would be riding the same winds as Columbus, supposedly. The trip to the Spanish Islands off the Americas were to take roughly two months, and that is what the captains supplied for. Once reaching the Americas, the real adventure would begin and the armada would have to head south, through Portuguese territory, around Brazil, and into the unknown latitudes of ice and snow. The ships were scheduled to set sail on the 26th of September, but not before Magellan had one last order.

J UAN SEBASTIÁN POINTED at the approaching vessel, and told Captain Gaspar de Quesada it was flying the Spanish colors. Still in the Canary Islands, the armada knew they were relatively safe. The arriving caravel was out of place, as many ships refused to sail alone in the heavily pirate infested waters, so near to Africa. Magellan had wasted no time meeting the captain of the arriving caravel. As soon as a communication pass down had finished, Magellan raised his flag, for all officers to report for orders.

Juan Sebastián looked around the Captain's table, at his fellow officers, who all sat dumbfounded at the orders they were hearing. Two Portuguese men-of-war had left Lisbon and were in route to intercept the Spanish expedition and destroy it. The armada would depart immediately, without

---

[17] Tenerife, and the Canary Islands in general were being used for centuries, as trading post for Africa, Portugal, and Spain. The slave industry and maritime industry were present here. The highest peak, Mount Teide, is nearly 14,000 feet above sea-level, and to this day acts as a significant aid to navigation.

waiting to finish supplying their vessels. In addition, to gain advantage over the pursing Portuguese navy, the Armada would head due south, beyond the Cape Verde Islands, and not follow the standard trade routes. Of course, Elcano and his other Spanish officers knew that the Portuguese were mostly interested in stopping Magellan, and securing his trade secret (his chart). The navy of Portugal would not dare attack Spanish ships in Spanish territory.

When Magellan than gave further orders on convoy positions and communications, the Spanish officers all knew their plans of mutiny had once again been foiled. Magellan had ordered all vessel to separate by the distance of the horizon, in a straight line, Magellan's ship being in the center. All ships would then match the speed of Magellan, close range at night and in storms, and communicate with simple fire-light signals and cannon-sound blast. This order of Magellan's showed how great of a strategist he was. By setting sail so quickly, sailing further south than anticipated, separating the crews, and forcing virtually zero communication between vessels, the Captain-General had avoided multiple possible attacks and mutinies. Juan Sebastián looked around the table at his fellow officers shaking their heads. Juan Serrano stood as Magellan stood and shouted, "Atención en cubierta!"[18] The armada would depart immediately.

 LCANO WAS NO STRANGER TO HUNGER. In the army, rationing was a daily chore. Aboard the Concepción, he was the officer in charge of

---

[18] For the leading authority, Magellan spoke little to his crew. Embarrassed by his thick accent, he would of relay orders through his subordinates. Once underway, Magellan became more vocal.

rationing. There was no cook aboard any of the Armada's vessels. The quality of food aboard these boats, mostly hardtack[19], rice, and salted pork, with a serving of wine, was such a low level, anyone designated as cook would have mostly likely been strangled. The position of "cook" was rotated when there was fresh food to actually cook, though being 45 days at sea, on the open ocean, there was nothing fresh about what Elcano was giving to the men.

The largest problem Elcano faced, was the crew's insistence to know their location. Juan Sebastián was a practical navigator and he knew they were located roughly half the distance they should have been, in the middle of the Atlantic. The other officers aboard the Concepción, including Captain Quesada, knew that the fate of the fleet was in a perilous condition. The men, they were sure that they would have reached the Bahamas by now, the Spanish Main even, all areas of the world many of the experienced seaman had traveled.

Magellan had ordered his ships further down the African Coast, missing the lazy trade winds that blow ships quickly across the Atlantic. What took Columbus 61 days to accomplish was now, on the average, taking ships 35 to 40 days. When the five ships left the Canary Islands in a rush, first having left Seville and then Sanlúcar de Barrameda in a rush, they were barely prepared for 40 days. Quesada held an officer's meeting at the end of that day. In this meeting, all aboard agreed that they were at least two additional weeks to the Americas, if the winds would pick up, but at their latitude[20], the trade winds were too far North. Magellan seemed to have led them into the doldrums, maybe purposefully endangering the fleet.

The Concepción's Officer Mess[21] unanimously agreed to break rank and signal the San Antonio. This was done and soon Inspector-General Cartagena had broken rank and began signaling too. Magellan could not have been happy, with so many of his officers openly betraying him.

---

[19] Compacted and Dried Flower

[20] Latitude was easily discernable by the sun at noon, date, and distance from equator. Time was important for this, and was an artform before the advent of maritime clocks nearly two hundred years later.

[21] Mess was originally defined as a group of sailors

∞ ∞ ∞

*I*T WAS HERE, IN THE BORED HUNGER AND SWEAT, that the pilot of the Victoria was found in a sexual position with one of the ordinary seamen. His captain, Mendoza, put the man in chains and signaled for the Captain-General. Magellan beaconed for his officers to muster aboard the Trinidad, where a trial was held for all to see. Within moments, the pilot of the Victoria, Antonio Salmon, and the cabin-boy, Antonio Ginoves, were found guilty of crimes and sins punishable by death. Antonio Salmon was bound with chains and escorted to the hold.

With an important figure needing to be replaced. Magellan ordered the Inspector-General's right-hand-man, Antonio de Coca, to the Victoria, to be the new pilot. Juan de Cartagena was not happy and he openly and vocally struck down Magellan's order. With no time to think, Juan Sebastián witnessed the Captain-General order the stewards to seize and arrest the Inspector-General. Juan de Cartagena was restrained in cuffs and taken back to the Victoria to be placed in the ship's hold, and watched by Mendoza and Juan Sebastián. Before nerves had calmed. The Captain-General issued a preliminary charge against both Antonio Salmon and the cabin-boy Ginovés. Salmon's charges were suspended until a trial could be had, and the cabin-boy's sentencing was to take place immediately, 100 lashes to be administered by the boatswain of the watch. The starving morale in the fleet was just penalized drastically, yet Magellan came out above – this time as a leader through fear and confidence.

With limited options, Magellan rearranged the crew once again, and placed Juan Sebastián back aboard the Conception, as the acting pilot of that ship, charged with helping the inexperienced Antonio de Coca[22].

---

[22] Not much is known of Antonio de Coca, other than he showed allegiance to Cartagena during the mutinies.

∞ ∞ ∞

$\mathcal{T}$HE LAND WAS ONE MORE POINT OF TENSION. They saw it. It's lush forest and cascading rivers. Birds. Marine-life. All waiting for the fleet. But Magellan would not stop. The currents were behind him, and he used the added push to move quickly away from the known Portuguese posts. Having made it across the Atlantic, further south than the regions under Spanish control, the fleet was in hostile territory. The officers reluctantly obliged, and the fleet followed the coast, at the ready for any acts of war.

Aboard the ships, temperaments were high. The Spanish officers were sure they were witnessing a rebellion. After the arrest of their comrade, Antonio Salmon, and the arrest of the Spanish commander, Inspector General Juan de Cartagena, Magellan appeared to be the man they all suspected he was back in Seville – a rogue actor or spy who had tricked the Crown into giving him his position and his fleet. Aboard the Conception, Juan Sebastián was busy discussing his options and orders with his new captain. Aboard the Victoria, with Mendoza, Juan de Cartagena was not about to be humiliated in such a way. The officers began to conspire to overthrow the Captain-General as soon an opportunity arose. They'd have to wait for a strategic moment, and in the mean-time, ensure they had enough support from their own crews.

As the ship skirted the coastline of South America, the crew was more busy than normal. Still hungry, the coastwise route forced more trimming of the sails (ocean going routes required almost no sail maintenance, and sail positions could remain stationary for weeks on end. Coastwise routes were tough labor for anyone in the rigs). The crew continued to struggle with hunger, even more so with the work. The land brought the presence of birds and gulls supplemented their diets. The routine, isolation and monotony brought illegal sex, games and conspiracy theories. As Elcano probed their loyalties, he did so with additional rations, and stories of the women in the Americas[23].

*O*N DECEMBER 13, 1519, Magellan ordered his fleet into a bay on the Brazilian Coast. Unbeknownst to his crew, Magellan secretly hoped the bay was the mouth to the passage he was looking for. Not totally unbeknownst to Magellan, the Spanish officers were scheming to overthrow their leader, the moment the opportunity arose. Magellan dispatched his ships to the corners of the Bay, soon to realize his hopes were unsubstantiated. The Bay had no large tributaries. Without the means to continue, Magellan reluctantly gave the order to anchor, knowing they were in Portugal territory. He would have to manage the situation smartly.

At anchor in present day Rio de Janeiro, the five ships began the process of finding replenishments. Elcano discussed his success in building a strong base of seaman allies with Juan de Cartagena. The two agreed a larger group of allies was needed, and to build such a group a subtle strategy should be developed. The idea to build bonds through morale was implemented. Elcano was no stranger to foreign women, and soon he was encouraging his men to have orgies with local women. Of course, hostages were taken. Pigafetta says that two young daughters were snuck into the fleet[24], and he

---

[23] Stories and myths from seafarers returning from the American Conquest were tremendously loaded with embellished nuisances. Every native American was a supposed cannibal. Every woman was a sex crazed beast. The difference in culture was so tremendously different, there was no vocabulary or literature present to understand such differences – hence the myths and mistaken communications between the two parties. Elcano would have heard more than his share of stories as a merchantman in Seville.

[24] There are zero accounts of Magellan taking advantage of women. There are also surprisingly no accounts of Magellan participating in any sexual act. The Captain-General had a strict rule of no unauthorized passengers, slaves, or women aboard his ships and he shunned any sexualization of non-Christian women.

writes that "The girls often came on board to offer sex to the sailors in exchange for gifts. In one instant, a girl stole a nail and hid it in her vagina"[25]

Seeing the unchecked fraternization of his men, amongst both officer and crew, Magellan saw the necessity to reaffirm his authority. A sentencing hearing was ordered, and the sinner Antonio Salmon, the pilot of the Victoria, and the whipped cabin-boy, Antonio Ginoves, were brought before their peers. Magellan allowed the cabin-boy to go free (which was due to his dying condition anyways[26]) and ordered Antonio Salmon to be strangled (an obvious signal towards the other rebellious officers in his fleet). His orders were carried out instantaneously and soon a line was tied round the neck of the pilot Antonio Salmon and his body was raised off the deck from the yardarm. Juan Sebastián was order to cut the lifeless body down and dispose of it.

Magellan once again, without warning, gave orders to set sail.

*T*HE FLOTILLA MOVED SOUTH, stopping again in Rio de Solis. It was here, as the fleet probed the Bay, and navigated the Uruguay and Paraná rivers, when the crews realized the Captain-General's chart was either wrong or non-existent. It was obvious. Magellan's crew was losing faith in their leader, and the Cartagena -Elcano movement for mutiny had gained enough members.

But Magellan continued to keep everyone on their toes. Despite the low morale. Despite the seemingly never ending probing the Coast for the mystical passage, and despite the freezing temperatures, and approaching

---

[25] Pigafetta, Antonio (see Bibliography)

[26] 100 lashes was a death sentence. The wounds from these lashes would be so painful many of the subjects would commit suicide soon thereafter (this is recorded in maritime and military history). Those who toughed it out, would die of bacterial infections, putrefaction, or other disease, including malnourishment – being unable to eat or drink with the inflictions.

winter, he gave orders again, to quickly set sail. With great reluctance, and much apathy towards their leader, the fleet left Rio de Solis. Elcano and Cartagena again, decided to wait it out.

∞ ∞ ∞

I T WAS IN THE HARBOR OF ST. JULIAN[27], Patagonia that Magellan gave the order to prepare for winter (southern hemisphere). It was March, 1520, and the fleet would have a few weeks to build the necessary supplies to winter. Gathering the needed supplies for 250 men was no easy task. A method of gathering and stowing food must be implemented. Fortified defenses for storage, protection and berthing would be built. The land would be searched. The locals would be Christianized. All of the rituals of conquer would be implemented, and the Spanish fleet would stake St. Julian as their own. And they would stay there until winter passed.

Juan de Cartagena would not wait. On the first of April, Cartagena was released by the Captain of the Victoria, Luis de Mendoza, and took command of the Victoria and the Concepción, under Captain Gaspar de Quesada. He immediately called on obedience from his friend and fellow officer Elcano and the Master of the San Antonio, Antonio de Coca. By April 2, three ships were commanded by Cartagena.

Without wasting time, Magellan sent a small group of men to give a letter to Mendoza. The leader of this group of men, the Armada's Master-at-Arms Antonio Fernandes, went aboard Mendoza's ship alone. With their guard down, Fernandes jumped on Mendoza and shouted to his men to take the ship. A bloody fight pursued and Magellan's lieutenant Fernandes came out ahead, and in charge of the ship. In no mood to be lenient, Fernandes

---

[27] St. Julian is the name given by Magellan. From this point forward, leaving the charted European territories, to the Philippines, all names are given by Magellan (so says Pigafetta).

plunged his sword through the neck of Mendoza, killing him in front of all the mutineers.

Now, Magellan maneuvered his ship into the entrance of the Bay, and anchored, blocking the exit of the other two ships. With three ships against two, the night set in.

Under the cover of darkness, Magellan sent a skiff to cut the anchor free of Juan de Cartagena's ship, the San Antonio. It drifted quietly towards the opening of the bay and soon the men of the Trinidad were able to raid the San Antonio and gain control. It was now four against one, the tables had turned. By morning, the mutineers were surrounded, with their exits blocked.

The quartered body of Mendoza was raised on the mast, by a close friend of the Captain-General, Duarte Barbosa. With fear and panic, the final ship, with Cabo, Quesada, and Elcano in charge, surrendered. The mutiny had been squashed.

∞　∞　∞

HE FOLLOWING TRIAL BROUGHT MORE DEATH. Gaspar de Quesada was sentenced in the style of the Spanish Inquisition. He was stretched out in the rigging. Thousands of pounds of pressure was created between his limbs and torso. His stomach was slit open, his body inverted, and his intestines and stomach were allowed to fall freely from his corpse. His body spasmed until it fell lifeless. It was then cut into portions, each of which was placed on a stake, which in turn were placed around the fortification St. Julian, as a reminder to all those who dared rebel.

Juan Sebastián and the fellow officer traders were put in chains. The subordinate crew were all released, freed from further inquiry, and encouraged to enjoy the land before the winter fell. Elcano and the officers were forced to work through the winter, reinforcing the buildings, salting meats and fish, barreling fresh water, and spinning yarns. They were given scraps to feed on. They shat in the corners of their dungeon like cells. They grew weak and infested with lice and soars. They awaited death sentences in the freezing months of Patagonia.

The freemen of the fleet were free and able to interact with the local natives, of whom they called giants. Again, Pigafetta notes the sex and orgies these men had. He also talks about the Brazilian hostages taken 9 months earlier, giving birth in this port.

And as the summer sun started rising, Magellan, doing what he did best, began making plans to sail, further Southward. Juan Sebastián Elcano was to live, to act as a pilot and to serve Magellan with no questioning, under penalty of death.

*T*HE SANTIAGO SET SAIL, under command of Serrano, with orders to scout the coast for the next harbor, and return once complete. It shipwrecked 20 miles from St. Julian, and all the crew members marched over the freezing mountains of Patagonia to return to the fleet and report the ship's demise[28]. The crew of the Santiago was split into fourths and the other four ships became crowded immediately. Serrano was given command of the Victoria and the San Antonio was left to Magellan's cousin, Álvaro de Mesquita.

Leaving St. Julian, Magellan thought it best to keep the morale up. The winter had gone fairly well, and the crews were rested, well fed, and ready to move towards Magellan's prize passage. There were still a few Spaniards who felt Magellan was in the wrong, and there were even more who believed Magellan lacked the knowledge he had sold their King on, but ultimately, the fleet was in as good as condition as ever, given the mutiny from months

---

[28] This trek would be a challenge for a financially sound mountaineer of the 21st century.

before. Magellan decided to maroon Cartagena and his brother[29], the priest Pedro Sánchez de la Reina. In August of 1520, Magellan set sail. While it was a known death sentence, it was not considered one in a moral or legal sense. As the fleet passed through the approach to St. Julian, for the last time, Cartagena and Pedro Sánchez de la Reina were left on a small island. They were given a small bag of hardtack.

As the four vessels headed south, they took a moment to collect as much as possible from the shipwrecked Santiago. With Magellan back in control, the women and even new "wives" of the men were all ordered to stay behind. The crews would have to focus to accomplish the task at hand.

---

[29] Juan de Cartagena had a brother, who was a priest, apparently, Pedro Sánchez de la Reina. The records are sparse on this point, as they are sparse on the point of Juan de Cartagena himself. It appears that it is not 100% proven that Cartagena was the illegitimate son of the Archbishop. If so, it would be fitting for him to have a brother in the function of the church as well.

The Passage

And so they remained there four days, waiting for the other two
ships. And during that time they sent out a well-provisioned
launch in order to find the cape of the other sea, and they came
back at the end of the third day and told how they had seen the
cape of the great sea. And the Captain-General wept with joy.
— Antonio Pigafetta

*J*UAN SEBASTIAN AND HIS FELLOW MUTINEERING officers were kept in irons, while they were not performing their watch-keeping functions. In exchange for their life, Magellan allowed them to pump the bilges and perform other manual labors. Their diets remained at minimum rationing levels, though the rest of the crew was allowed to eat as much as they could, as the ships were now expected to travel only in view of the shore.

On October 21, 1520, the devout leader of the Armada de Molucca was celebrating the Saint Ursula and the Eleven Thousand Virgins, and it just so happened a bay was entered at latitude 52 degrees south – to be forever known as Cape Virgins[30]. Europeans had never been so far south, so far as anyone ever logged and lived to share. At roughly 12,000 miles from Spain, as the crow flies, the Armada de Molucca had crossed nearly double that distance over water, avoiding the Portuguese, scouting the coast, tacking back and forth with the wind. It was only one more bay, one more reason to work hard for most of the crew. For Magellan, it was potentially his saving grace. If this bay turned out to have a passage west, he could buy more time

---

[30] Cape Virgenes

with his officers. After the previous year, it was hard to convince them that he knew where he was and what he was doing. Magellan had told his closest associates he had only been charting the coast as he went south, to ensure a thorough report could be given to the King upon return. This new bay showed promise, though at least one Captain did not think so.

∞ ∞ ∞

FOUR SHIPS ENTERED THE STRAITS leading to the Pacific Ocean. None of them knew where they were, or that indeed they had entered a strait. There was no clear sign of fresh water[31] and there was no obvious sign of an end, though there was also still no obvious sign of an exit or a large body of water on the far side. The bay they entered turned into narrow channels, and fjords. The fleet went slow, charting each inlet and each turn with precision. With a bit of luck, the normally hostile environment of the Strait of Magellan was relatively calm, with few storms and little fog.

For weeks the fleet continued their efforts. The fear of the unknown, the spooky fires in the hills[32], and the myths being passed through the decks were starting to shake the confidence of Magellan's men. During officer meetings, many suggested the fleet should turn back. That they had done enough, discovered enough, and would be heroes if they returned to Spain at this point. Magellan refused; confident he had found what he was looking for.

---

[31] Fresh water would suggest the inlet was only the mouth to a river, and not a passage to another sea.
[32] Tierra del Fuego has kept its name for 500 years.

∞ ∞ ∞

THE VESSELS WERE ORDER TO DIVIDE into two groups, and take separate paths forward. Orders were given to search, record, and return to a specific spot within a week. A week later, the San Antonio, the fleet's largest ship, filled with the most supplies, was gone. An entire ship, full of unreplaceable goods and foods, including trading materials and livestock, was gone. Juan Sebastián knew the lower ranking officers aboard, and knew that the ship had deserted, and would be on its way back to Spain. But Juan Sebastián kept his mouth shut. His friend Esteban Gómez would surely spread the story of Magellan's rogue and cruel methods. Juan Sebastián was happy the San Antonio had gone. Magellan, however, did not know this. The San Antonio may be in need of assistance. Maybe it is lost, or shipwrecked. Magellan's friend, Álvaro de Mesquita, was the commanding officer onboard, and Magellan must have been concerned for his safety. If a mutiny had transpired, Mesquita would need help. The order was given to search for the vessel, and two week later the voyage resumed, resigned to the loss of its second ship. Now the crew was down to 150 men, and three ships.

By the end of 38 days in the passage, on November 28, 1520, 350 miles of westward travel, a salt water bay was spotted. And to Magellan's relief, and to the great shock and disbelief of the crew, the far end of that bay was another ocean. They had found the passage through the New World. They were successful, for the first time since setting sail from Seville, a year early. They were successful!

Magellan now needed the skillset of open water navigators. Juan Sebastián, after taking a second oath of allegiance to the Captain-General Ferdinand Magellan, was brought out of his irons, and tasked with keeping track of their location on the globe. Astronomers[33] and mathematicians had calculated the ocean, at the far side of the New World, to be about 500 miles wide, and they were counting on the Armada de Molucca to verify their

---

[33] Astronomy was not a thorough science at this point. Like all science from the 16th century, it was heavily, if not totally, burdened by religion, superstition, Greek mythology, and guess-work mathematics.

equations. Magellan would have to ensure they measured every step accordingly. Also, he'd need to be able to retrace their steps on the way home.

After his redundant pledge of allegiance, Magellan gave Juan Sebastián a gift, a luxury item that only the noble class would have had access to, and a premium delicacy such a long way from home, a jar of jam.[34]

∞ ∞ ∞

EFORE SAILING INTO THE OCEAN, Magellan took inventory. If all was correct, he was a few weeks from the Spice islands. He'd need complete obedience from his crews. He'd need to be ready for Portuguese men-of-war[35] . He'd have to be ready to be successful. Without the San Antonio to carry extra supplies, in its larger holds, the ships were ordered to over stock their stores. Magellan allotted a few days for the crews to hunt and gather herbs and water. The holds were filled with salted mussels and any local mammal meat that could be found. It was disappointing for the crews to find that the stores of raisins, figs, and almonds had been either depleted, contaminated by rodents and weather, or taken by the crew of the San Antonio.

Before sailing into the ocean, Juan Sebastián rubbed his wrist and filled his stomach. Surprised at Magellan's success, Elcano felt doomed. The busy ships were not enough of a distraction for the officer. As he pulled out the few charts he had, and limited knowledge of the globe, he felt a shallow emptiness. The Pacific Ocean would go by quick and all of the promises of Spice, Silk and Gold would be true[36]. He had betrayed his King by betraying

---

[34] This quince, jar of jam, is the reason most officers on sailing ships never experienced scurvy, like their subordinate crew. It wasn't until Captain Cook, in the 1750s, started to correlate nutrition with scurvy that the dilemma was figured out. Before that, it was a matter of social status and luck.

[35] Man-of-war: a vessel readied for battle.

[36] The greatest minds influencing European navigation in the 15th and 16th century never came close to grasping the size of the Pacific Ocean. Maps of the globe, prior to Juan Sebastian's return were incomplete with a small body of water between Asia and the Americas. They were also full of speculated islands of wonder and probable monsters guarding them.

Magellan, and the paradise they were discovering would not be shared with him. When the fleet made it back to Spanish territory, he'd be labeled a traitor and sentenced to death. All he could do was wait until that moment, make his captain happy, and hope for forgiveness.

As the Armada de Molucca left the coast, by the Straits of Magellan, it headed North first, to the latitude Magellan knew the Moluccas were on. From that latitude, they'd head due west, into the blue. Neither Magellan nor Elcano knew this small rise in Latitude[37], would prevent the Armada from spying much needed islands as they headed west. Historians have gawked at this little twist of fate, that cost Magellan so much suffering.

---

[37] It would have benefited Magellan to stop in Argentina and the Chilean coast, but his site was only on the Moluccas, at least in that instance.

Crossing the Pacific

3 Months of Salt: 1520/1521

They sailed out from this straight into the Pacific Sea on the 28th
of November in the year 1520, and they were three months and
twenty days without eating anything, and they ate biscuit, and
when there was no more of that they ate the crumbs which
were full of maggots and smelled strongly of rat urine. They
drank yellow water, already several days putrid, And they ate
some of the hides of that were on the largest shroud to keep it
from breaking winds. And they softened them in the seas for
five days, and then they put them in a pot over the fire and ate
them and also much sawdust. A rat would bring half a ducat or
a ducat. The gums of the men swelled over their upper and
lower teeth, so that they could not eat and so died. And
nineteen men died from that sickness and the giant together
with the Indian from the land of Brazil.
— Antonio Pigafetta

$\mathcal{J}$uan Sebastian Elcano's new calculations were correct. Ferdinand Magellan knew this. But the fleet was not nearing land. The bottom was unfathomable. Wildlife, kelp, and debris was not to be seen. Ocean swells were evenly spaced and far apart[38]. They both looked through the vast accumulations of written knowledge mariners had been compiling

---

[38] Sea-life, marine debris, and swell are just a few examples of nautical objects mariners can use to roughly judge distance from land.

for centuries. The works of Marco Polo. The journals of Spanish and Portuguese explorers. Notes from Balboa (the first European to see the Pacific). Charts created by astrologers, mathematicians and the church. When all that humankind knew failed, they resorted to the Bible. Stories of lost paradises, giant creatures, seafaring tragedies. Other myths combined with tales. Were the monsters, creatures and dragons real[39]? Was there an end to this vastness? Weeks with nothing. Endless blue. Blue sky. Blue water. Blue eyes. Blue horizon. Blue reflections. Everything the same. The sun comes up and it all turns blue. The sun goes down and the sky fills with the same fires they saw in Tierra del Fuego. Everything the same.

Below decks, unlike the officer class, the men slept on hard wooden planks. Without racks or bedding, washrooms, heads, or basic hygiene practices, bacterial infections were wide spread. The order to begin heavy rationing was a surprise to the men. Before that, they were sure their leader had a map to Ophir. Their spouts of excitement mixed with boredom and suffering were reprimanded harshly with whippings, confinement, and even execution. Magellan pushed for prayer service to be held multiple times a day. Pigafetta took to work of converting the captives the Armada had brought from Patagonia – the giant and other native Americans, all who would die first of scurvy or starvation.

In the officer's circle, there was much talk about turning around. Magellan had found the straits. Wasn't that enough? Elcano fantasized about returning to Spain. The San Antonio would be there, and the King's men would be on the docks, ready to arrest Magellan for treason. His passage to nowhere was not useful to Spain. The value of the ships and the honor of the Spanish sailors were truly what he was obligated to, under his birth right to Spain. But maybe the hunger was getting to him. Maybe he was beginning to act like the crew, crazy. He buried himself in his chores, his compass, and the celestial orbits of every strange star he could find – none of which were the stars he knew back home[40].

---

[39] It's now collectively thought Arabian Spice traders guarded their trade routes by telling elaborate spook stories. Some of the earliest maritime charts from the Arabian Sea include iconic images of sea monsters, dragons, and death symbols.

[40] The equator and shorter lines of latitude were known as early as 15th century sailors. Determining your location north and south of the equator was relatively

As the vessels strayed west, world grew larger and larger. The knowledge humans knew they knew, grew smaller and smaller. Magellan and Elcano both wondered what they were getting into, and if they'd live to share their experiences and their new sense of size with their loved ones, with the Kings of Europe.

∞ ∞ ∞

HE WINDS HAD DIED. The tillermen could push and pull at leisure without affecting the ships course, though they were exhausted and couldn't stand the thought of doing such a thing. Every piece of sail was up. The three ships drifted without purpose. One over there, a few miles off the port, the other, on the horizon off the bow. All the sails sat motionless, as still as the sea. The blue around them was just blue, sky and sea. A man died at some point on the Victoria and there was talk of sharing his body. Magellan lashed the man who suggested it. That man died.

There was an officer in the crow's-nest of the Trinidad, not Magellan, not Elcano. The silence and blue in which he was watching was disturbed by the sudden plume of smoke from the Victoria, at least 15 miles away. Before he could yell to the boat bellow, the ferocious cannon blast overtook the Trinidad in the loudest sound any of her crew have ever heard. A second blast came roaring by. The signal. "Land ho!" "Land ho!" "Land!"

There was no way to maneuver directly. Magellan ordered the launch the skiff with ten of the liveliest crew. Each with soars on his hands, from working the sails for a year nonstop, now pulled on 75lb, twelve-foot oars. "Stroke!" "Stroke!"

Magellan would not dare leave his ship. He sent Juan Sebastián. The objective was to report to the Victoria, collect a team, and take two skiffs to whatever had been sighted. They would then judge to return to the ships then, or make camp and return to the ships the next day. A small ration of

---

simple. Compasses were also accurate by the 15th century. Still was that pesky problem of not knowing how big the world was.

hardtack and dried meat was given to the skiff. The crew each took a ration of water before they left – they would replenish water on land.

∞ ∞ ∞

*E*LCANO'S REPORT WAS THAT THEY WERE UNLUCKY. And the name stuck: "The Unlucky Islands." Puka-Puka was uninhabited when Magellan's fleet landed. Elcano had suspected such before he rowed out from the Victoria, but he didn't want to give anything less than all he could to Magellan. He wanted no reason to be quartered, to be split into four bloody pieces. When the first skiff hit land, a man ran through the sand, splintering his bare feet on pieces of coral. He fell to his knees and sobbed like a child. Elcano threatened the man, to return to the skiff, and he did so. The two skiffs sat on the white sand atoll, amazed at the lack of wave action. The ripples on the shore were too small to make a sound. There were no birds. A pile of sand and coral, not much larger than a yard within Castilian Castle's walls, surrounded by blue. Three distinct white sails on the horizon, all pointed in their direction, though none with any sort of drift. Elcano shot a single shot, "we are returning." Sounds of insanity could be heard coming from the man with bloody feet. Elcano ignored it.

The following day three men died. The atoll was no longer in sight. It appeared that the fleet was drifting further west, but it was not due to a wind.

Neither Elcano nor Magellan knew that Puka-Puka was about half way across the Pacific Ocean. The currents and little wind were sucking them North West, and the heat grew day by day. On the 60th day at sea, January 21, 1521, the remaining good food was gone. A spoiled barrel of hardtack was opened, and Juan Sebastián was ordered to issue rations at the same rate. The spoiled hardtack was soak in rat urine and droppings. The officer began to buy rats from the crews. Crews began to sneak salt water and boil the leather (ox hide) covers from the sails. The officers and Magellan ignored the ridiculous efforts to survive.

"Wind ho!" They heard the cry, but Elcano and Magellan felt no wind. They looked over the rail, in the direction of the Victoria and the Concepción, and they saw them with tight full sails. Soon, the Trinidad was pushing water at a rate of 6 knots. They had crossed the Equator, and the wind was finally driving them. The largest question stopped being where the wind was driving them, it became when it would get them there. Any place would do.

$$\infty \quad \infty \quad \infty$$

THE ACCOUNTS VARY FROM 19 TO 30 MEN. Though at roughly 150 men to leave South America into the Pacific, both numbers are significant and place the death rate at 1 every 3 days or so, or 20% dead. With sails full of wind, and desperation in the air, Magellan separated his fleet by horizons. The Trinidad in the center, slightly ahead, and the Victoria and Concepción on either horizon, port and starboard. This line of vessels moved almost due west, stretching nearly 100 miles apart, with a view of nearly 200 miles from north to south, sweeping the Pacific for land. By the 80th day, men were dropping every day. The bottom of the spoiled hardtack barrel was a pudding of virus, and the men fought for who was eligible for another serving. Juan Sebastián kept order with relative ease, as the men were too weak to fight. The tillerman was always given an extra serving of hardtack, from the officer's hidden supply. Elcano, Barbosa, Serrano and Magellan boosted their hardtack with quince, and they were not losing teeth like the men.

On day 97 marine mammals were spotted. Giant unmoving clouds in the distant marked the possible tops of mountains. The abundance of fish and sea debris was noticeable. The following morning, the officers convened, and it was generally agreed land was to the north of their location. China maybe? Some place unknown? On the 98th day, a massive land mass laid on the Trinidad's bow. Magellan ordered the rations to be lifted, and for the men to help themselves to the bottom of the barrels.

Once anchored, it took moments for small sailing canoes to approach the ships. The men in these canoes were darker than the Europeans. They brought spears, and larger pearls. Yelling and hollering upwards, over the bulwarks at the bedazzled Europeans.

Barbosa and Serrano would go ashore first. This was not the first time these men had encountered strangers in a foreign part of the world. The exercise was routine, if it wasn't for the despicable state of hunger Magellan's men were in. There only objective was to only bring back a full cask of fresh water, and, if they were fortunate to find anything, something edible for the crew. They disembarked on March 6, 1521 with a dozen soldiers, on present day Guam, 99 days after leaving the Coast of South America.

The island was full of "thieves," as Elcano noted to Magellan. Like mice running from a flood, the islanders scurried over all the sides of the ships, too many to fight off. Magellan's men were left aloof and without energy to defend themselves. The islanders stole gear directly out of the rigging, and they stole skiffs, swords and tools. The master at arms on each vessel yelled orders to stop, though none would dare raise their weapons without Magellan's approval. Magellan himself, was busy trying to negotiate with some random islander. He had no intention of starting a fight, with the condition of his men. He'd have to stay alive long enough to get resupplied, then he could go after his property.

The vessels took minimal replenishments. A few water casks each. Food was pillaged from a nearby village: grains and meat. Magellan gave his men a full day to recover. They then sent an army of 50 soldiers to retrieve their goods. Juan Sebastián was among these men.

As they ransacked the nearby village, protected in iron armor, and with muskets, the vessels at anchor volleyed cannon shot into the surrounding hills. Those natives that could not run, the elderly and children, were left to burn as Elcano set his fires. The men found were slaughtered[41]. The women, after being raped, were slaughtered too.

---

[41] The Pigafetta account of this list only 7 men. Though we know from similar accounts, including Pigafetta's, that the number was more likely higher, and that he deaths of elders, children, and women did not tally the same as men capable of fighting.

As the fleet set sail, the billowing smoke had attracted additional sailing vessels from other villages. Elcano was in awe of the number of naked savages and boats that responded. He wasted no time and asked permission from Magellan to unleash the cannons on the boats as they departed. Magellan agreed.

∞ ∞ ∞

T THIS POINT IN THE EXPEDITION, no officer knew what to expect, or where to travel. Judging by the stars, Magellan anticipated correctly that he was near his destination, though he wasn't sure of how far. The technology and language of "The Island of Thieves" was nothing like that of the Spice Islands. Which meant he was not close. He set a course with the information he had, keeping a slightly tighter formation as they headed south-southwest. In just over a week, land was spotted again. This time, the vessels headed for an island near Samar, in the Philippines. They dropped anchor and went ashore, much more prepared than when they reached the Island of Thieves. It was March 16, 1521, and the Magellan expedition was nearly a thousand miles from their goal, and they would quickly realize this when Magellan's slave[42] Enrique started speaking with the native king[43].

---

[42] Historians differ on how they label Enrique. Some use "indentured-servant." Some say he was paid, and therefore just another cabin-boy. Ultimately, he was stolen from his home of Malaysia, sold to Magellan, and was forced to work through both fear of life and promise of freedom. He was a slave.

[43] The kings of the Philippines would have been more exposed to traders than their subjects. This fact alone vouches for their ability to speak and understand more languages. This is an important concept when determining if Enrique did indeed complete a circumnavigation.

Magellan's Success

Elcano's Doom

The Captain had him told that if God granted that he return
again to this part of the world, that he would bring so many
men, that they would completely subjugate his enemies, and
that he had to go to dinner. And that afterwards he would
return to set up the cross on the top of the mountain. They
replied that they were happy. Our men shot of their muskets,
and then the Captain embraced the kings and the chieftains,
and took his leave.
— Antonio Pigafetta

*E*LCANO WAS AT FIRST JUST AS EXCITED as the rest of his fleet. They apparently had made it. Enrique was speaking his native tongue. There was kindness amongst the islanders. Everyone was ready to trade. Food and water were abundant. But then he remembered his conundrum: if Magellan succeeded, he would surely be tried and tortured for treason.

Magellan was beside himself. He acted like a God! He'd found the passage. He'd apparently made it around the globe with three of his ships. He'd survived four mutinies (one more was remaining). He'd survived over three months of the most passive seas anyone could image. He'd gained the trust of his men and his enemies. The islanders he was encountering either loved him, or were easily smashed. He felt invincible. And in this mode, he did what any God fearing Catholic would have done. He focused on his thanks and praise to his Christian Savior. He would give thanks for his success, by finding souls for his God and for his King!

∞ ∞ ∞

HERE WAS NO CONTRACT WITH THE SPANISH crown to convert natives. Elcano and Joao Lopez Carvalho, Elcano's superior Spanish officer, discussed the incentives Magellan had. There was no incentive to barter with the pathetic locals over titles, lands, or goods. The fleet had made it. Their orders were to map their route, load up on spices, and return uncaptured. Magellan was losing his grasp on reality. But it wasn't just Magellan. Barbosa, Serrano and Pigafetta had bought into it as well. The crews were allotted time with the newly Christianized women, so they bought into it too.

For weeks Magellan island hopped, forcing the inhabitants to convert or die. To swear allegiance to the King of Spain, or suffer the consequences. Tribe after tribe, village after village, fell to Magellan's armored men. Their crossbows and swords and loud cannons struck fear into the inhabitants, and most caved to Magellan's demands without a fight. Each and every new beach or island the fleet arrived at, a war party with Magellan leading the way dealt the inhabitants death or salvation[44]. Magellan's success and leadership style were earning trust, loyalty and respect from the men.

Pigafetta and the men howled in cheer and gluttony. They fell to having orgies with the local women. Pigafetta noting much details in his journal. Juan Sebastián, not surprisingly, participated in the sexual acts, when he was permitted to go ashore. The entire party was distracted from the mission, and the holds of the vessels remained mostly empty of spices.

---

[44] It should be acknowledged that Magellan was truly a good leader. Both in the Portugal conquest in Indonesia and with the Armada de Molucca, he fought alongside his men, he set moral standards and stayed true to them. He showed compassion with lower ranking seaman, and he refused to take hostages, unless his scientific counterparts thought it would be of use to the King.

∞ ∞ ∞

O N MARCH 17, 1521 THE FLEET LANDED at Cebu. The King of Cebu, Rajah Humabon, admired Magellan from the start. The two held parties and talked religion, trade and conquest. King Humabon organized a mass christening, and in the course of an evening, 800 natives were converted to the one true religion. As Pigafetta and most of the crew enjoyed the hospitality of King and his now baptized women, Juan Sebastián began his new plan, going from crewmember to crewmember and probing their allegiance.

If enough men were to support Elcano's idea, they could sabotage one or two of the ships, while their shipmates were ashore, and sail into the distance. Once on their own they would find the Moluccas, load their ballast to the brim, and head back to Spain. Elcano reinforced the appeal of such mission, as he would allow any members who joined him to keep a box of cloves for themselves[45]. This, he knew, would be difficult, but the promise would have been tough to turn down.

On April 25th, Elcano and Magellan were both present when the King of Cebu asked for help defeating his enemies on a neighboring island. The island of Mactan. The deal was made, and Magellan laughed at the thought of conquering another island for Spain. At this rate, Magellan would have all of the Philippines Christianized and under allegiance to King Charles.

To reinforce his support, the King of Cebu had his tribe build a massive cross above their village, which would overlook Magellan during his battle. The King gave a final warning, that this enemy was ruthless, and not typically open to negotiations.

---

[45] A sock of cloves would allow a single family to retire, and live comfortably. Cinnamon, nutmeg, cloves, and mostly any spice, would offer wealth beyond imagination for any of the crew of fleet.

Juan Sebastian Elcano reserved his plans again. He was used to being patient, and, at the rate things were going, it would just be a matter of time before Magellan slipped. Elcano would be ready.

The Armada de Molucca made plans for another battle. This time, they would be going a short distance, as a favor for their new friends in Cebu.

Magellan's Death

Elcano's Luck: April 1521

*The Captain-General sent the Moor to Cilapulapu to ask if he
wanted to obey the King of Spain, and recognize the Christian
king as his lord and pay him tribute, and he would be his friend.
If they wished otherwise, they should wait to see how our
lances wounded.*
—Attribute the quote

The entire fleet departed Cebu on April 27th. Anchoring in the cover of
darkness, Magellan mustered his officers to make plans. Juan Sebastián was
quick to volunteer, in hopes of possibly gaining more loyalty from his
Captain-General, but when he asked for 100 men and trickery with the
cannon, Magellan refused. Magellan proclaimed that there was no possible
way they could lose. And that one European could fend off 100 islanders.

Magellan laid out his plan. With three skiffs, they would land two parties
on the beach, while the third boat stayed off shore within ranger of
crossbows and archers. If worse came to worse, the third boat would lay
down covering fire as the first two boats retreated.

As the skiffs approached their destination cove, the enemy tribe, under
the King Lapu-Lapu, rushed the shore with hundreds of men, shouting jeers
and raising their primitive wooden clubs in the air. Magellan was
embarrassed for them. He ordered his skiffs to the beach. As they rowed
closer, an unseen reef was blocking the progression of the party. They would
have to go in one at a time, and leave their archers out in the bay, too far to
be effective.

The vessels proceeded. Pigafetta was in the bow of the second skiff, giddy with the process of seeing his beloved Captain-General devour the heathen islanders. They would surely pay for their cocksure attitude.

Magellan's craft landed and he ordered his men to form a wall. Ten sailor-soldiers, clad in heavy iron armor arched around their skiff, as Magellan raised his two hands in the air. "Praise be to God." His slave Enrique repeated: "Worship our God."

Pigafetta's skiff hit the surf hard and spilt onto the rocky beach, smashing his head in the process. Now nearly 20 Spaniards and Magellan stood tall, with swords, and shields at the ready. The islanders wasted no time and they began to pummel the intruders with rocks and spears. Magellan could not believe what he was seeing. He ordered an advance, which worked momentarily. He elevated his sword and pointed into the direction of the supposed leader. A second barrage of spears and stones was hurled.

Magellan ordered a fire to be set, at the nearest buildings, and he moved his wall of men to open an avenue for his soldiers to carry out the order. Running across the beach with torches in hand, three of Magellan's men took a heavy beating, one being impaled by a thrown spear. When they made it to the first house, the flames engulfed the dry brush roof instantly, and the inhabitants swarmed the three soldiers and began the process of beating them and removing their armor. Magellan reacted with a cry to fight. His men unleased their fear and anger and raised their swords. The islanders also began to charge; first in an ordered fashion, a single man at a time. And when the isolated islanders appeared to be giving Magellan's crew damage, more charged. Within the count of a few minutes. Magellan's wall of men began to collapse. The men were fending off multiple attackers apiece. Magellan shouted to regroup, "Regroup!"

Pigafetta had clambered to the gunwale of his skiff and was pushing it back into the waters. The third skiff, remained past the breakers, out of firing range, and had little interest in rescuing their shipmates or leader who was being overrun. Pigafetta's skiff floated and he jumped in. Moments later he felt bodies piling on top of him. When he was able to crawl to the rail, the five men in the boat with him were pulling on the oars as hard as they could, they barreled directly through the oncoming surf.

Pigafetta realized Magellan was not with him. He stood up and turned towards the beach. At that exact moment he saw an islander strip off Magellan's helmet. With a spear in his chest, the Captain-General raised an arm to block the oncoming blow, but his arm was not strong enough. A hard-swung mallet broke through the guard of Magellan's arm and landed a direct blow to his temple, knocking the mammalian brain of Magellan into eternity.

∞ ∞ ∞

THE TRINIDAD, VICTORIA, AND CONCEPTION were anchored with their rails fully manned. The respective Captains on each ship, Barbosa, Serrano, and Carvalho, as well as Espinoza and Elcano, all were in as much shock as their crew. Juan Sebastián raised his binnacle in time to see Pigafetta hysterically screaming at the rowers, who in turn jettisoned him overboard. On the beach he saw islanders dancing and holding pieces of armor high in the air. Then he noticed the armor was full of flesh. Of the twenty men who departed for battle, five were on a skiff returning, and Pigafetta was in the water swimming, soon to be picked up by the skiff of archers.

∞ ∞ ∞

WATCHING THE SCENE JUAN SEBASTIÁN was horrified. This surely would mean more battle. Magellan was dead, but his friend Barbosa and Serrano would be out for revenge. They'd at least want the body of their leader. But, if nothing else, this would be the beginning to the end of this absurd stop of these worthless islands.

Once the quiet fell, the main thought of the men, now without their fearful master Magellan, was to regroup to safety. But Barbosa and Serrano wasted no time, and the following day a negotiator was sent to Lapu-Lapu for the release of the body. The negotiator came back empty handed.

Testimonies from this point are shaky to say the least. Though it seems that the fleet agreed to return to Cebu, to seek advice and help from their newly baptized brother, King Humabon. The King was not pleased, and worse, he was now in a worse off position than when the Europeans had arrived. With his enemy, Lapu-Lapu, victor over the Europeans, he would surely attack the Cebuano village.

Meanwhile, aboard the Trinidad, Elcano witnessed Barbosa and Serrano whip Enrique. Enrique was wounded from fighting beside his master Magellan[46]. And though he was loyal to his master, his master had given Enrique his freedom, if he were to die. Knowing this, Enrique refused to obey the order of the new captains, which were for him to negotiate with the King of Cebu for help. When Enrique declined, he was beaten into submission.

E NRIQUE RELUCTANTLY HEADED TO CEBU. There he met with King Humabon. Beyond initial Christian greetings, there is no record of what transpired in that meeting, other than the King was notably irate. Enrique certainly communicated something specific, as a time and place were agreed upon, for the new European Commanders to meet the King for a feast and discuss the plans which the Europeans had.

Serrano and Barbosa went to King Cebu, alongside a small group of armed men. There they anticipated a feast, possibly and orgy, and continued loyalty

---

[46] Most accounts agree that Enrique was beside his "master" throughout the voyage, both in good and bad times. On the beach of Mactan, Enrique was not only acting as translator, he also fought beside Magellan, and was possibly the last to leave the beach and survive. In any case, he was wounded to the point of demanding rest from the new European commanders.

to the Spanish Armada. Despite losing their beloved hero, Ferdinand Magellan, Serrano and Barbosa were both excited at the prospects of being the new leaders of the expedition. The events of the past few days lifted their spirits, and a celebration was what they needed. They were the honored guest, and center of attention for once. Enrique even said the King wanted to offer precious ornaments and supplies.

The fleet's ranking Master-at-Arms, Gomez Espinoza and the fleet's leading Pilot, Joao Lopez Carvalho, saw their situation in a different light than their two leaders. Completely outnumbered, both Espinoza and Carvalho left the celebration in order to "get presents for the King." The truth was that they planned on returning with more armed men, in case the festival turned bloody.

The unthinkable soon happened. As Espinoza and Carvalho rowed towards the nearby anchorage, they heard the cries of their colleagues. A flood of Europeans was seen running for the water, then the natives came out of the surrounding woods with cries of war. They watched their men falling on the beach, barraged with spears and stones. As Elcano pulled Carvalho aboard the Concepcion, they heard Serrano scream for help. Their new Captain-General was surrounded on the beach.

Carvalho ordered the cannons to be unloaded on the beach and the village, but with Serrano wrapped in rope and bound on the beach, the crew wouldn't dare annihilate their own leader. The cannons did not fire. From less than 100 feet, the crews of the Armada de Molucca once again watched their leader die from the murderous blows of natives. Serrano begged to be spared. He shouted orders to the ships to bring bargaining aid. He was torn limb to limb, and the King of Cebu was seen delivering a death blow, while Enrique stood at his side, passive and almost smiling.

Carvalho became the Captain-General[47] by default, and he raised his sails without consulting his fellow officers. The fleet left Cebu, after days of suffering and defeat, and headed with the wind towards Indonesia, closer to their goal.

---

[47] The ranking within the fleet was not crystal clear, at least not after the mutiny back in St. Julian. With a majority of the leaders dead, and the fleet reduced to a few officers, the ranking officials were easier place. Carvalho, without a doubt, was next in line, even if he was not the best for the position.

∞ ∞ ∞

HE FLEET WAS REDUCED TO THREE SHIPS and less than 100 men. The success of the previous weeks had vanished and anguish and terror were spreading through the men. Joao Lopes de Carvalho took command of the fleet, and soon developed a plan with Elcano. They would scuttle the Conception, and continue to the Spice islands with the Trinidad and the Victoria. Juan Sebastian would thus forward be the master and captain aboard the Victoria, and Espinoza would retain control of the Trinidad. Carvalho would demand the title of Captain-General, replacing Magellan and the Barbosa and Serrano duo.

Carvalho proved to be a weak leader. As they recklessly navigated their way around the Indonesian waters (the Malay archipelago) for six months of wandering – to Borneo and Mindanao, he pirated every ship it encountered. From these ships he would demand the pilots give direction to the Spice Islands. The rules and order aboard the ships had collapsed, and multiple reports survived of the surviving men taking native captives, mostly women. The Natives in the Indonesian Islands were appalled. Espinoza could not control the men aboard his own ship, with such a reckless and poor leader as Carvalho.

Juan Sebastian Elcano felt the opposite of Espinoza. Like Carvalho, he too was in a state of euphoria. The Portuguese bastard Magellan was out of the way. His loyal kin folk and Portuguese friends were mostly dead from the Battle of Cebu. He was roaming near the famed Spice Islands with a ship of his own. His Captain-General was a poor leader and nut-case, but he was Spanish. All Elcano had to do, was enjoy life, fill his holds with spices, and sail home. Everything else was apparently falling in place. Besides, he was now the only and irreplaceable navigator aboard, as Carvalho had received his position through status and not skill.

Elcano did not know Carvalho would lead the men into another battle. With the fleet down to two ships, and chaotic navigation, the Armada de

Molucca was not at the ready for any hardships. When they reach Brunei, that's what they found, all thanks to Carvalho.

∞ ∞ ∞

*B*runei was going to bring a bad end to the fleet, and worse for Carvalho. Having captured a pilot aboard a Chinese Junk, they were led to the island to meet King Siripada, a Muslim Spice Trader. The crew and Carvalho were completely enthralled by the King and his island of riches. However, the King had assumed that the white sailors were from Portugal. When he learned that they were actually the enemies of Portugal, he ordered their Armada sunk and hostages taken. Carvalho, Elcano and Espinoza fought their way free from the onslaught, though Carvalho had abandoned his son while fleeing. Elcano and Espinoza elected to overthrow the rule of Carvalho, and Espinoza became the new Captain-General, completely reliant on Elcano for navigation needs.

Heading south, away from Brunei, a merchant vessel was boarded which had a captain onboard who knew the way to Ternate and Tidore. On November 6th, 1521, the fleet saw their goal in the distance. And landed on Tidore on November 8th. 1521. With Juan Sebastian Elcano and Gonzalo Gomez de Espinosa as the Armada's surviving leaders, Spain had successfully, beyond an arguable doubt, completed a course west from Spain to the Spice Islands[48].

---

[48] It's true that many of the officers within the fleet knew they were near the Spice Islands from the point of landing in the Philippines, and certainly when they landed in Brunei. Though, having physical evidence, and seeing known and charted landmarks was a comforting piece to the mission. The pressure release felt from reaching Tidore was from multiple angles. They could now return home 100% successful.

∞ ∞ ∞

$\mathcal{T}$WO MONTHS WOULD BE MORE THAN ENOUGH time to pack the holds of both ships. Two months was too long for Elcano's calculations. Monsoon season would affect the travels in either direction of departure, and Elcano wanted to leave as soon as possible. Likewise, Espinoza wanted to get word to King Charles that the Armada de Molucca had been successful. It was then agreed that the two ships would part ways. Elcano would volunteer to continue west, towards and around Africa. Espinoza would transit backwards, retracing Magellan's route, and cross the Pacific. They should reach Spain at the same time, and if one arrived sooner than the other, it could send help.[49]

Espinoza had to stay with 51 men to fix the Trinidad before they sailed east. Elcano, with 47 men were to continue west, immediately. Within weeks the ships were replenished with stores, water and food. Their holds were filled with the best spices of the era – cloves and nutmeg.

On December 21, 1521, the Victoria, under command of Juan Sebastian Elcano, departed the Spice Islands, separating the Armada de Molucca in to two, to return to Spain via Cape Horn. Gomez Espinoza wished the Captain well, and cannons were fired as the two ships parted ways. Elcano knew that Espinoza was in no condition to navigate across the Pacific, and he also knew the season was not correct for such travel. He kept his mouth shut and wished Espinoza and his men well.

---

[49] This help would happen. It was the Loaísa expedition, ordered by King Charles in 1525. The purpose was to colonize the Eastern Spice Islands, and retrieve all missing crew from the Elcano Expedition. Unfortunately, of the seven ships of this fleet, only one made it, and that crew was in no condition to assist anyone. Though Loaísa searched for the Trinidad in the Straits of Magellan and on the Coast of South America.

∞　∞　∞

*E*SPINOZA WAS NO MARINER. Aboard the Trinidad, he headed east during the worst possible time. With monsoon seas in full effect, the 52 men onboard had no chance. The water intrusion from above decks alone spoiled the dry storage within weeks. A 1000 miles into the Pacific, Espinoza was forced to make a U-turn and head back towards land. The Trinidad was now taking on water from below, and his scurvy ridden men could not keep up with the pumps. Worms had completely destroyed the Trinidad's hull.

As they approached the Moluccas, a Portuguese fleet surrounded the Trinidad, and it was surrendered. Antonio de Brit, the commanding officer, noted less than 40 men, all dying from exposure to the sea. All 40 men were imprisoned, and only four survived to see Europe again, years later, including Gomez Espinoza.

.

Crossing the Indian

Elcano's Leadership

In order to round the Cape of Good Hope, they sailed to 42° of south latitude, and they remained in the vicinity of this cape for seven weeks under sail, with headwinds from the west northwest, and with storms. This cape lies in 34°, 30' of south latitude, and sixteen hundred leagues from the Cape of Malacca and is the largest and most dangerous cape in the world.
— Antonio Pigafetta

P IGFETTA SAID NOTHING OF JUAN SEBASTIÁN ELCANO, not even for the entire half of the expedition that Elcano was the Captain of the Victoria and Captain-General of the voyage. The two must have spoken on the year long journey home. In that time, Pigafetta must have been tormented by Elcano's good fortune. Likewise, Elcano must have been concerned about Pigafetta's journal. Did Pigafetta's journal originally include Elcano. Could Pigafetta have removed Elcano under some bargaining condition?

Within months, from the Isles of Thieves, to success at Cebu, to Mactan where Magellan stopped breathing, Juan Sebastian Elcano saw his demise flip into triumph. All he had to do was focus and motivate his men. Make it to Spain. And stick to the story which shows he did everything he could for the King of Spain. He would be a hero!

We know Juan Sebastián 's story even without a description from Pigafetta. The first published account of the entire circumnavigation actually did not come from Pigafetta. Antonio Pigafetta's story was translated and given to royalty across Europe, though were not published publicly until the 1530's, nearly a decade after the adventure. The first published accounts were government inquiries into the surviving crew. In his "De Muluccis Insulis," Maximilianus Transylvanus records the narrative from the perspective of three survivors, days after landing. Juan Sebastián Elcano, Francisco Albo, and Hernando de Bustamante were all among the interviewees to this report. Also, we can infer much from Elcano's past. As the younger brother, he was in a mediocre spot in the family maritime trade business. His skillset for navigating was amazing, but the repetition of the routes and subordinate role beside his brothers was more than a buzz kill. Moving onward to the army, he was still in a subordinate role, though now he had men under him. His pay and his position brought out a reckless side. He could have women with ease, many women. He could eat lavishly, live above his means, rack up debt. Then his return to Spain, after the wars, he used his new military status to acquire a ship and business. He was the boss and the owner. His ship made some money, though it wasn't enough. The power was satisfying, though he wasn't getting ahead.

Then the spiral happened. With mostly low and lowering points, though with the occasional silver lining. The Genova bankers busted him, and confiscated his ship to pay off his debts. The Spanish government locked him in jail for losing his ship to the Italians. He bartered with the government, receiving a pardon, in exchange he'd work as a lowly officer aboard a fleet of ships sailing under the orders of a Portuguese traitor. This position was an embarrassment, and also a borderline death sentence – sailing into an unknown part of the world statistically was a mortal decision. However, embarrassing and risky sailing was better than 16th century prison. He then met Juan de Cartagena, and learned that there may be a way out, by overthrowing the Portuguese Captain-General. This gave Elcano hope, and that hope built until Magellan split the Elcano and Cartagena at Sanlúcar de Barrameda.

The long and dull trip across the Atlantic. The mutiny he participated in, with an exciting 24-hour period followed by sudden and drastic despair. His colleagues were dismembered, strangled, whipped, and marooned. The hard-toiling labor in South American snow and ice. The bruises from the chains and the hunger.

Magellan's success in Patagonia, the discovery of the mythical passage. The horrid conditions of the Pacific Ocean, death and pain on every plank. Magellan's status with the crew. Their success in the Philippines. Thousands of baptisms. The circumnavigation. Each and every moment of Magellan's success was a dagger to his chance of survival. Every day they neared a successful return to Spain, was another nail in Elcano's coffin. He'd be mauled by the King and his dogs. He was a dead man – but he'd have to be tortured first.

Then it happened. Magellan died. Then his moronic friends followed suit. Then with spice-treasure spilling out of their ballast and onto the decks, his new leader, Carvalho, made a grave error, and Elcano was promoted to the captain and commander of his own ship. If the Victoria knew the fate of their sister ship, the Trinidad, and fate of their new Captain-General Espinoza, they would have known that the Victoria was now the sole surviving ship of the fleet of the Armada de Molucca. Juan Sebastian Elcano was the Captain-General of the first Armada to sail around the globe, and he was just over half of the way there.

As for Juan Sebastián Elcano – the feelings of success have hardly been felt by anyone so strongly. Not only about what he was about to accomplish, but that level from the depths of despair he was just days prior. When he lands in Spain, he'll be saluted by everyone. He'll be the first around the globe. His knowledge will be praised by all the scientist. His conquest will be praised by the King and the King's men. His treasures will bring him and the expedition's creditors great wealth. He'll be able to retire with Noble privileges. Who knows, maybe the King will give him land and titles.

That first day under wind, from the Indonesian Islands, he stood on fantail, staring at the world he was about to encircle, and he smiled. What a glorious moment for him and his family. The peaks of Tidore would soon dip beneath the horizon. His men would need to stop once more, somewhere well clear of Portuguese outpost.

∞ ∞ ∞

J T WAS JANUARY 23, 1522, Victoria's last stop, Timor, in the Southern Indonesian Islands, roughly 3000 nautical miles south of the Philippines and another 1000 nautical miles north of the then unknown Australia. Juan Sebastián would have known a rough estimate time of arrival for the Vitoria in Spain. Between the Italian Journalist Antonio Pigafetta, the Portuguese Pilot Francisco Albo, and the Spanish Navigator-Captain Juan Sebastián, the educated mariners aboard the Victoria knew at least that they would be at sea for two months.

The routes around Africa, across the Indian Ocean, were all under Portuguese Territory. The Pope himself declared this[50]. If his ship was discovered, they'd have to out-run whoever chased them. If they were captured by Portugal, everything would be done for. They'd become prisoners of war, an outcome that in all probability would lead to their deaths. Juan's Sebastian could live with himself if he lost men to hunger. He would not live if Portugal found him. He set his course to compensate for the threat. The Victoria would travel further out to sea, more south. They would bypass the opportunity to replenish on the Indian and African Coast. They would set a course directly to the Cape of Good Hope.

At this point they would have had a rough calculation of the size of the globe. Their system of longitude would be stable enough to set a course within a degree or two of their destination. The charts and locations of the Portuguese trade routes were all brought on the voyage by Magellan, and left for everyone when he died. They were not however privy to Elcano, and they remained with Espinoza. On a ship weighing nearly 85 tons, stretching 65' long, and damaged from four years of hard sea-going life and worms, the crew was weary of the trip. At the onset of their journey, they had 55 crew onboard, shoved in every nook and cranny. Now, with most of their crew

---

[50] Treaty of Tordesillas, 1494

dead or missing, their cramped quarters were even more so, due to the mass supply of dried cloves and nutmeg.

A strict food and water regiment would have to be implemented immediately. Minimal crew would be used for operations, and the rest would be required to stay quiet and out of sight. A tillerman, a lookout, navigator/pilot, and boatswains' mate and a Master-at-Arms would be the only duties on the crossing of the India Ocean. Every ounce of energy would be needed for when the Victoria approached Portuguese shipping routes near Cape Hope, and along the west coast of Africa. One facet of 16th century carracks were their ability to keep course with minimal effort. The sails and rigging, according to records, were often left in place for three weeks at a time, not needing any work.

Once again in the middle of the ocean, and unknown body of water, Elcano and his men faced boredom, fear, and lunacy. It would not take long for their limited diets to affect their nervous systems. It was not unexpected that the 13 Asian captives onboard (from Timor) started dying first.

*D*EATH SWEPT THE DECKS OF VICTORIA. It was May, and by all previous calculations, Cape Agulhas or Cape Hope should have been spotted by then. Elcano had missed something. The sun and the stars all said that they were hundreds, maybe even a thousand, miles from the nearest land mass. The primary currents (and thus winds) sweep the entire Indian Ocean in a giant counter clockwise circle. When Elcano decided to avoid Portuguese shipping lanes, he put his ship into head on winds and currents. As he crept slowly closer to the Southern Latitudes, to pass Cape Hope, he entered into stronger currents, now being pushed by a combination of the Antarctic Circumpolar Current and the Aqulhas Current. By the time land was spotted, near the vicinity of the Cape Agulhas[51], almost 15 of the crew of the Victoria were dead. Juan Sebastián had learned a valuable trick from Magellan, to stow a secret supply of food and water, and to share that supply with your most valuable asset – Francisco Albo, the Pilot – and to encourage your working crew with when times got rough. Unfortunately for Juan Sebastián, his time at sea would surpass the brutal 99 days at sea Magellan and the three ships experienced a year earlier in the Pacific. As the crew gawked at the tip of Africa, as they surged through 15 to 20-foot seas, their stomachs were feeding on themselves. Their teeth were falling out daily. But the pounding headaches, diarrhea, and mad-rants would all stop immediately with the slightest fall or injury. An injured man would not be spared, if he could not do his required work he'd be discharge overboard. A bleeding man risked bleeding out, as the nutrient free diets prevented the body from healing itself. It had been 117 days since the men had last seen land.

*P*ASSING THE CAPE OF GOOD HOPE on May 19, 1522, Victoria sailed North. In wind and storm, once again creeping to sea for days, weeks, then tacking back up wind toward land. Trying to stay far enough to sea to avoid any Portuguese ships. The men begged to head towards the nearest port. Elcano denied them this. When death transpired, the crew refused to throw over the bodies, but Elcano forced to do so.

No one questioned why Elcano and Albo failed to get sick. They were hungry, starving too, though they had energy the other men did not. Their teeth remained in their skulls. They were not covered in their own vomit,

---

[51] Cape Agulhas is the Southernmost tip of Africa. Cape Hope is the safe harbor nearly 100 miles north east of the tip. The two are commonly confused as one landmark.

sores, and blood. Their daily rations were being supplemented with Elcano's personal stores. Pigafetta did not receive this same kindness.

As the men died around the holds and decks of the ship, so to the slaves. The last slave woman, raped to her dying day, was thrown to the sea – "sinking face down," Pigafetta noted. Juan Sebastián ordered Pigafetta and Albo both to stand work rotations, in the rigging and on the tiller. Juan Sebastián himself took to hard labor, steering the ship.

May came and went, the entire month of June was a blur to those who survived. By July, Pigafetta could not write, nor had he anything to write. Juan Sebastián's secret food supply ran out. The men who were previously scolded for stealing from the cargo, were now free to do so – not that it mattered. Dry cinnamon, nutmeg and cloves were useless without water.

The Cape Verde Islands were approaching, and a known Portuguese outpost was there. The crew had no choice, and Juan Sebastián agreed, they would have to stop, or die. As they approached the port, sailing skiffs approached them. They lied. They said they were merchant men, lost at sea, in need of supplies. The Portuguese were suspicious, though were disgusted by the condition of the men. They agreed to allow the Victoria to anchor, and they even allotted barrels of hardtack and fresh water to be exchanged. On July 9th, the first transport skiff was enough to vitalize the men. The second was enough to boost everyone's spirt. The third skiff was sent ashore, and it did not return. Elcano thought the worst. He knew if he left, he may not make Spain – his ship needed repairs and they should still take more supplies. On the other hand, the port had multiple Portuguese Caravels that could arrest the Victoria, and end the expedition before it reached Spain. Elcano choose to leave. In doing so, he left five men ashore, doomed to become prisoners of Portugal[52].

Heading north, Pigafetta, Albo and Elcano were all confused by a piece of knowledge they had learned in port. Their ship's calendar was wrong. Not just the calendar of any one man, but everyman had a record that was one day off. This bit of information may have been more valuable than all the Spices, though it became nothing more than a nuisance to the crew – as they

_____

[52] Elcano was correct is suspecting the Portuguese were onto his scheme. The men of the third skiff that went ashore were arrested almost immediately, and through simple questioning of the starving men, the cover had been blown. The Portuguese would soon depart Cape Verde and chase the rotting Victoria to Spanish waters.

were most likely worried about celebrating their holidays on the wrong day. It was not long before the Victoria crossed the route she had made nearly three years early, just after departing the Canary Islands. At this moment, near 22 degrees north and 23 degrees west, with over 20 original crew onboard (the 4 slaves did not count), the first circumnavigation of the world by one ship was complete. Though nobody on board thought to celebrate this[53]. It would take 30 more days to reach home.

Unfortunately, Victoria was not riding in the sea well. She was springing new leaks daily, and plugging holes was not sufficient. A 24-hour pump rotation was established, and by August the 20th, a two man dewatering station was set, to operate all day and all night. This exhausting rotation was manned by crew that could barely speak, due to lack of energy and pain. Elcano reinforced the assignments each crewman had through a whip and threat of being jettisoned overboard or chained, or all three.

By early September the coast of their home could be viewed on the horizon. Just a day or two and they'd be free. Two more men would be dead by the time they made land fall.

On September 6, 1522, 14 days shy of three years, the Victoria, with 18 original crewmembers docked, to an awaiting crowd of armed Spaniards, officer of the courts, and hundreds of shocked civilians. Only Juan Sebastián Elcano and Albo did not faint once the lines were on. The remaining crew collapsed on the decks and were carried off the ship to the docks. Within hours, the Victoria was secured from threat of sinking and her cargo was inventoried. 4 slaves and 52,000 pounds of spices was the official prize.

Elcano sent a message immediately to his King. The Armada de Molucca was successful, and the Captain Juan Sebastian Elcano had brought the King the only remaining ship.

---

[53] No one has ever celebrated this. Ever.

Circumnavigation Complete

Juan Sebastián Elcano: 1522

Primus Circumdedisti Me.
(You first encircled me.)
—augmented inscription on Elcano's coat of arms

SEPTEMBER 6, 1522 MARKED THE LANDING OF VICTORIA in Sanlúcar de Barrameda. The King was sent a message instantaneously. And preparations to ship the Victoria up river to Seville were made[54]. On September 8th, 1522, the remaining crew of the Victoria moored in Seville Spain. Surrounded by 100s of citizens, come to see if the rumors were true, that the Armada de Molucca was successful, the ragged crew crawled to their feet. Draped in fresh white sheets, the men followed their leader, Juan Sebastian Elcano, through the city to the Victoria's namesake, the El Convento de Nuestra Señora de la Victoria, in the neighborhood of Triana[55]. There, in the presence of the people and authorities of Seville, Juan Sebastian Elcano thanked God, and El Convento

---

[54] Coastal cities were vulnerable to both piratical raids and hostile takeovers. Most global navies and their cargoes were kept safe inland, where practical, to prevent these burdensome events. The trip to Seville would have included fresh men, and many of the ship's crew were already discharged – probably abandoned to the gutters. It's doubtful that these men had managed to keep any spices, as once promised by Elcano.

[55] The historic church suffered fire and demolition by various groups over the past five centuries. In 1950, anything original that remained of the building was bulldozed to give way to new buildings.

de Nuestra Señora de la Victoria, for all the success of the Armada de Molucca.

It did not take long for rumors, that the crew of the San Antonio had arrived a year earlier, and had called Magellan and the other Portuguese Officers "traders." The crew of the Victoria was all gathered and asked not to leave Seville, until a proper interrogation could be made. Pigafetta paid his respects to King Charles by giving him the original copy of his journal[56].

Elcano confessed that there was a mutiny in St. Julian. That he believed that Magellan may have had dual motives, and that many of Magellan's close associates may have had dual motives (only Espinoza would make it back to Spain to defend himself, from behind bars). With the testimony of both the San Antonio and Elcano, Magellan's rights were removed. His wife and children were not given their share of Magellan's earnings. And they were ordered to remain in Seville, in case additional information arrived. The name Magellan became a curse for the Portuguese for centuries[57].

The mixed stories and scandalous accusations were suppressed by the Spanish government, and by the Casa de Contratación. Juan Sebastian would be a hero, though he would agree to remain in Seville, at the insistence of the crown, and he would repay any past sins by committing to the Spanish cause. His family would be granted land rights in the Philippines. His coat-of-arms would be scrubbed, and the insignia "You First Encircled Me" would belong to his family from that moment onwards.

Within day, Elcano and Albo were requested by Maximilianus Transylvanus, an investigator sent by King Charles, to take the stories of himself, Francisco Albo, and Hernando de Bustamante. Pigafetta is notably left out of this interview, perhaps because he had already passed over his journal and left Spain. Within a few days he published "de moluccis insulis" (the Molucca Islands), directly to the public. The headlines were that Juan Sebastian Elcano was the hero, who made the Armada de Molucca a success.

---

[56] Which has not been seen since.

[57] This is true. Though with the influence of the Pigafetta accounts, Magellan soon became a heroes' name. Because Spain was claiming Elcano, Portugal began to claim Magellan. Because direct copies of Pigafetta's journals were distributed throughout Europe, by Pigafetta himself, it was only a matter of time before Ferdinand Magellan would have the title of First Circumnavigator, by the rest of Europe.

Hero Elcano

Death at Sea: 1526

The next day Antonio Pigafetta went to Valdoli where the
Emperor Charles was in residence. And he did not present him
with gold, silver, or any other precious thing worthy of so great
a lord, but with a book written in his own hand, in which were
set down the things that happened from day to day during their
voyage. And from there he left to go to Portugal to King Joan,
and told him the things that they had seen, the Spanish as well
as his own people.
— Antonio Pigafetta

D ESPITE HIS FAME AND FORTUNE, Elcano was still indebted to the Holy Roman Emperor, King Charles V. When Spain decided to send a fleet to claim the Philippines and the Eastern portion of the Spice Islands, the newly established Council of the Indies, directed by none other than the still Archbishop, Juan Rodriguez de Fonseca, Juan Sebastian Elcano was the top choice to manage the navigation of the fleet. Elcano saw it as both a blessing and his demise. First, it would allow him to lay claim to his lands in the Philippines, under the authority of a major, seven ship Spanish armada. Second, he knew that the Pacific lay in wait. There, that brutally blue sea, would most probably destroy them.

The Loaísa Expedition, commanded by García Jofre de Loaísa, was more than just an expedition to colonize. It was designed to completely steamroll through the tip of South America, laying claim to those lands there. To scope out routes to the Western side of South America. To discover depots in the

Pacific Ocean. To show force to the Isle of Thieves. And to colonize the Philippines and the Eastern Spice Islands. If that all worked out, they would also be in a good place to rescue their missing friends from the Armada de Molucca.

∞ ∞ ∞

O N JULY 24, 1525, AFTER ELCANO had successfully left his blood line in the children of two random women in Spain[58], the Loaísa Expedition departed Spain. Juan Sebastian would be the lead navigator.

By May 26, 1526, the fleet arrived at the far side of the strait Magellan had discovered six years earlier. Still no other Europeans had been there. There were no signs of the Trinidad[59]. The Loaísa fleet had lost two ships in the Straits, and one more deserted. At the urging of Elcano, the fleet spent a prolonged time preparing for the crossing of the Pacific.

The Pacific was not pacified this go round. The fleet of four were separated in a never-ending storm. One ship ended up on the Mexican coast, which was lucky. Another ship vanished completely[60]. A third shipwrecked on an island where the crew was killed off or enslaved[61]. The fourth ship made their target in the Philippines.

Arriving in horrid conditions, this fourth ship, Santa Maria de la Victoria, was quickly taken captive by a Portuguese Armada. The 25 survivors were jailed for almost a decade, and returned to Europe in 1536.

---

[58] He also left a will naming these children.

[59] The happenings of the Trinidad would not be unraveled until the two survivors returned to Spain in the 1527 – one being Gomez Espinoza.

[60] The galleon San Lesmes was never heard from again. However, many Spanish Maritime artifacts liter the Pacific Islands, few dating back to the early 16th century. Steel was found in the Sandwich islands by Cook, who assumed the Spanish had been there.

[61] Four of these men were saved by another Spanish Armada years later.

Juan Sebastian Elcano would watch the commander of the expedition die of starvation aboard the Santa Maria de la Victoria. Elcano would take charge for a few days. Though he was in bad order. Deranged with putrefied gums, ulcer covered skin, his brain degenerated into mush. In early August, 1526, Juan Sebastian Elcano would retire his command, and die aboard the Santa Maria de la Victoria, a month before it made landfall in Indonesia.

His surviving relatives, brothers and children included, would eventually make their way to the Philippines, years after Elcano's death, to lay claim to the hero's prize.

The End

The First Eighteen

The First Ones to Circumnavigate

We already know why it's wrong to say just one man was the first to circumnavigate the world. We also know why it's wrong to claim Magellan was that one man, or Magellan's slave Enrique was that one man. If you missed it, we only know this for sure: the following men set sail under Magellan in 1519 from Spain and they returned with Juan Sebastián Elcano, having circumnavigated the world before any other humans had done so. These 18 men were the first, in alphabetical order:

Antonio Hernández Colmenero
Antonio Pigafetta
Diego Carmena
Francisco Albo
Francisco Rodrigues
Hans of Aachen (Agnes)[62]
Hernándo de Bustamante
Juan de Acurio
Juan de Arratia
Juan de Santandrés
Juan de Zubileta
Juan Rodríguez
Juan Sebastián Elcano
Martín de Judicibus
Miguel
Miguel Sánchez
Nicholas
Vasco Gómez Gallego

---

[62] This man also survived the Loaísa Expedition. The first man to circumnavigate the globe twice.

Bibliography

If I could recall every source of information I've ever devoured on this subject, I would give it due credit here. Below, are only the books and papers I have in my collection. They certainly influenced my writing. Within my book, only the names and specific dates did I look up, and the internet was the quickest tool I used for that, never using one specific source of information, and never taking another's work without due citation. Please remember, I wrote this because it is a point of view that should be available to everyone, not just those who can read Spanish. This text is not scholarly; it has not been peer reviewed and I do not meet the citation requirements of most academic papers. This book is however, a tool to bring you closer to the truth of The Elcano Legacy.

Juan Sebastián Elcano: La Mayor Travesía de la Historia: BibliotecaOnline; 1 edition. May 13, 2018. eBook.

Kelsey, H. The First Circumnavigators: Unsung Heroes of the Age of Discovery. Yale University. 2016

Morison, S. The European Discovery of America: The Southern Voyages. Oxfor University Press. 1974.

Múgica, S. — Elcano Y No Cano. Online. 2019

Mundle, R. Captain James Cook. ABC Books. 2013

Pigafetta, A: Magellan's Voyage Around the World: Sagwan Press. Print. August 24, 2015.

Pigafetta, A. The Voyage of Magellan: The Journal of Antonio Pigafetta. Translated by Paige, P. William Clemens Library. 1969.

Zweig, S. Magellan. Pushkin Press. Print. January 10, 2012

About the Author

Bradley Thomas Angle

The maritime offers perfect platforms to monitor social phenomena, with both formal and informal methods. We can look at maritime history for a peek at what to expect in all the realms of social expectations: Globalization, Religion, Sexuality, Culture Exchange, Social Progress, Technology, Environmentalism, Politics, etc. Boats are laboratories and sailors rats.
—Dirty Sailor Company

This is Bradley Angle's second full length publication, the first being Shipmates: Before the Mast. As a career mariner, and a boisterous academic with a love of beer and dogs, Bradley spends his free time orchestrating a website geared towards expanding the knowledge mariners have of their own industry, history, and culture. Dirty Sailor Company seeks to use social happenings in the maritime to explaining social phenomena in other situations.

Juan Sebastian Elcano was a character Bradley learned of when he first studied the "Magellan Voyage." Like most Americans, he never thought to question the incomplete circumnavigation as anything important. In a twist of fate, Bradley's girlfriend scheduled a trip to Seville in 2019, 500 years after the Magellan expedition departed there. He soon learned that Spain celebrates Elcano, and not Magellan.

Made in the USA
Coppell, TX
09 February 2023

12533364R00056